Praise for Matt Murray's

THE FATHER AND THE SON

"This is a riveting and tender memoir, a shining testament to the human spirit and our need to find meaning in our lives. I could not put down *The Father and the Son*, and its cadence and rhythm stayed with me long after."

—ABRAHAM VERGHESE,
author of *My Own Country* and
The Tennis Partner

"In the current glut of memoirs, this one is extraordinary. The history of a beloved father's journey into monastic life told by a cool-eyed, unsentimental son is both objective and sympathetic, critical and compassionate. The power of Matt Murray's book lies in his understanding of the admirable yet sometimes inexplicable choices his father made. It is written with the kind of affectionate restraint one rarely encounters in these emotionally hectic times."

—DORIS GRUMBACH

"Matt Murray's writing is direct, forceful, and moving. What I liked best about his memoir was a thrilling honesty as the youngest member of a family looks at the other members and his parents, and himself, in the family constellation, watching, often impeding, moments of understanding, and often misunderstanding what others think and feel. The depth and quality of the work make it stand apart from so many children's memories as they contemplate their parents."

—JOANNE GREENBERG,
author of *I Never Promised You a Rose Garden*

"What makes people join a monastic order or enter a convent? Do they hear voices, as Joan of Arc did, or see a blinding flash of light like St. Paul? *The Father and the Son* is an intensely personal memoir suggesting that religious vocations are borne out of convictions that have deepened and clarified over a lifetime. . . . *The Father and the Son* is a courageous book; in describing the long germination of his father's religious vocation, Murray reminds us that other things—like a son's understanding—also ripen beautifully with the passage of time."

—*Los Angeles Times*

"This is the old story of a son's search for his father, dressed up in a monk's cowl and told with the pace of an adventure thriller. It's a journey well worth making."

—*USA Today*

THE
FATHER
AND
THE SON

THE FATHER AND THE SON

My Father's Journey into the Monastic Life

MATT MURRAY

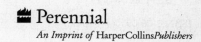

Perennial

An Imprint of HarperCollinsPublishers

A hardcover edition of this book was published in 1999 by HarperCollins Publishers.

HarperCollins books may be purchased for educational, business, or sales promotional use. For information please write: Special Markets Department, HarperCollins Publishers Inc., 10 East 53rd Street, New York, NY 10022.

First Perennial edition published 2001.

Designed by Eric Coates

The Library of Congress has catalogued the hardcover edition as follows:
     Murray, Matt. The father and the son : my father's journey into the monastic life / Matt Murray. — 1st ed.
       p. cm.
   ISBN 0-06-018782-4
   1. Murray, James. 2. Monks—United States Biography.
  I. Title.
  BX4705.M9765M88   1999
  [B]271'.102—dc21   99-34165

ISBN 0-06-093067-5 (pbk.)

01 02 03 04 05 ❖/RRD 10 9 8 7 6 5 4 3 2 1

Listen carefully, my son, to the master's instructions,
and attend to them with the ear of your heart.
This is advice from a father who loves you;
welcome it and faithfully put it into practice.

THE RULE OF ST. BENEDICT

You know how it is with fathers, you never escape
the idea that maybe after all they're *right*.

JOHN UPDIKE, *Rabbit, Run*

ACKNOWLEDGMENTS

Authors these days are increasingly appending long, meandering acknowledgments to their books. Here are mine.

Both for the original article and for this book, a number of friends and relatives of my parents were generous with their time and input and helped me tap into places and events beyond my ability to imagine. They include Ken and Joyce Murray, Leonard Murray, Marie Wolcott, Peter and Carol Halfon, Marion Garmel, Joanne Greenberg, Lori King, Bud Foote, Jerry Wilson, Paul Fuqua, Jim Lardner, Donald Graham, Mary Ellen Aubrecht, Rita Tybor, Clifford Ridley, and Clare Levy.

The monks of Saint Bede Abbey, and especially Abbot Roger Corpus, OSB, deserve special thanks for their support of this book and their willingness to open up.

Thanks too to my brothers, David Murray and Jonathan Murray, and my sister, Sarah Murray, who shared memories and reflections and offered me support. I owe a special debt of gratitude to Sarah for editing my mother's voluminous journals down into a useable manuscript years ago, and for sharing with me old family letters that were in her possession.

This book grew from a story that appeared in the *Wall Street Journal* in June 1995. Thanks for that story are due first and foremost to Carol Hymowitz, who was a strong backer of the article from the beginning. John Brecher, the *Journal*'s Page 1 editor, was enthusiastic and encouraging about my attempt to write a personal, first-person narrative in a space usually reserved for stories about failed mergers and Latin American trade crises. John also assigned as my editor on the story Ron Suskind, whose advice and insights shaped the original article and continued to prod me as I wrote this book.

Thanks to the support of Paul Singer and Dan Hertzberg, who gave this book the go-ahead and Clare Ansberry. Steve Adler provided feedback on the manuscript.

Mary Evans, my agent, was a believer from the beginning and a strong advocate to the end. At HarperCollins, Robert Jones, my editor, brilliantly edited down the mass of mush I presented him seven months late. Fiona Hallowell, his assistant, answered 10,001 stupid questions for me. Thanks, also, to Eric Steele, Philip Hening, and Tanya McKinnon.

Among the friends and colleagues who read, commented upon, and muted any private criticisms about the manuscript were: Janine Flory, Bob Mazzoni, Patricia Davis, Greg Ip, Nancy Nantais, Elizabeth MacDonald, Deborah Lohse, Nancy Keates, Kim Narisetti, and Raju Narisetti. My thanks to all of them—and apologies to anyone left out.

Finally, thanks to my father, though they seem barely sufficient; after all, this is his story, and he generously gave it to me in dozens of hours of interviews, and in a thousand ways over three decades. I hope I have done it some justice.

PART ONE
THE SON

ONE

※ ※ ※

The year I turned thirteen, my father declared himself the patron saint of frustrated housewives. From the time I started ninth grade, I lived in constant danger of coming home from school to find a group of his disciples gathered in my living room. I would tromp up the front sidewalk, jiggling my keys, whistling or humming, kick open the front door, let the screen door slam shut behind me, drop my backpack to the floor with a thud—then turn and discover I was a virtual intruder in my own house.

Five or six of my father's followers would be seated in a little circle of chairs. All were housewives from the neighborhood, women in their late thirties and forties whose husbands were at work. Their eyes would be focused adoringly on the only man in the room, a middle-aged figure with graying temples, a bushy mustache, a slight paunch, and an aura of sincerity: my father.

Dad presided from a large leather recliner. Though dressed in around-the-house clothes—a cotton short-sleeved shirt, jeans, slippers—he composed himself with the authority of a judge in a robe. He sat up straight, hanging over the edge of the chair. His eyes were closed, his cheeks flushed, his frame tensed.

The surrounding scene resembled a séance. The front curtains were drawn, leaving the whole room shadowy. The group held hands. Sometimes I could hear someone mumbling, but I could never tell whose lips were moving. The only motion I detected came from a flickering candle on the coffee table. Even the dust particles seemed suspended in the air. In the stillness, it felt like everyone had stopped, breathless, waiting for something.

But not for me. My invasions never registered with anyone. I was like a character in a ghost story who can see and hear those around him while they are completely unaware of his presence. No one's head would turn at my entrances—not even my father's.

The women were members of Dad's new prayer group. He had begun hosting them several afternoons a week that autumn. Until that year, I had never heard of a prayer group, hadn't even known that people bothered to pray outside of church. Over the next few years, I managed to grow accustomed to them.

But I never could quell the gnawing unease my father's new hobby stirred up inside me. I missed the way things had been before he fell in with these people. I resented them for taking over the living room and banishing me to my bedroom so many afternoons. I disliked catching a glimpse of my father in such an intimate, private act as praying. From where I stood across the room, he seemed so isolated, so far away from me and everything around him. Most of all, I worried that he was starting to like being with them more than with me.

The women had quickly come to fill his days. Though he was now in his early fifties, he was acting like a teenager trying to become popular with the in crowd. I, the real teenager, felt like a tolerant parent as he babbled on about the gang over dinner or in the car. Every day there was a new joke, a funny story. Reluctantly, I came to know all about their lives. One, he confided, had a troubled marriage. Another had a violinist daughter who attended the Juilliard School in New York. This one had a rail-thin husband with a nervous tic that made his head jerk slightly to the left. That one foisted loaves of home-baked bread on us, heavy doorstops of dough.

I could see the tenderness my father felt for them was reciprocated. The women seemed to find in him the rare sensitive man to whom they could bare their souls and from whom they could receive encouragement. They called him on the telephone for advice. They invited him for bike rides in the park. They joined him in the morning for mass, then came back to our house with him for quiet talks over coffee.

They were friendly enough to me. They always asked me about school. But I found it easy to resist their Christian cheer and unassuming openness. To me, the women were a vivid outward sign of changes occurring within my father that I sensed were taking him away from me. They brought out the worst of my adolescent sullenness. It wasn't personal; mostly I was just annoyed with them for accompanying him on a journey I did not want to take myslef. And so as much as possible I kept them at arm's length. I told myself they resided in a strange world where I did not want to live.

Over time, I compiled questions for the lot of them, questions that flooded my brain whenever they came to my house: Where are your husbands? Do they wonder about this man you spend so much time with? Do you have romantic intentions toward my father? Don't you have homes of your own? Silently, I would interrogate the women as I crept past them to get a snack from the kitchen. Silent but brilliantly, I cross-examined each as I passed back through on my way to the stairs, cookies in hand. I grabbed the banister like a life preserver. Only when I was up in my room, with the door closed and the television turned up loud, did I find sanctuary.

Lying on my bed, I'd listen for the sudden eruption of life downstairs. Soon the quiet was broken: Conversation started up, chairs scraped the floor, good-byes were exchanged at the door. The house emptied out. Finally I heard the front door shut definitively behind them.

Only now came the rhythmic scuffle of slippers on the stairs, the clanging and jangling of the metal crosses that my father had taken to wearing around his neck. I'd lie there and listen to his plodding tread as he climbed the steps. He would knock on my door, then pop his head inside before I had granted him leave.

"How you doing, bud?" he'd ask.

And around me, I could feel the house begin returning to my custody. For a while, anyway.

✦ ✦ ✦

At the beginning of 1979, my father, James Murray, was fifty-two years old. He was a widower of five years' standing, a still-handsome man who went on two or three dates a week, a well-regarded government bureaucrat with a high rank and good salary, the owner of a tidy, two-story home in Bethesda, Maryland, a moderately successful playwright, a father of four, and a profoundly unhappy man.

Only the last trait was not readily apparent to the outside world. Despite the hole my mother's death had left, to most colleagues and old family friends he seemed a vigorous man in the prime of life. He radiated warmth, possessed a self-effacing sense of humor, and carried himself with an appealing modesty that was dignified yet inviting.

But within our family, some of us worried that he was a man whose spirit was slowly seeping out of him. He seemed to be sliding into a premature dotage. He was defined less by what he had than by what he had lost.

Just a few years earlier, Dad had held a high-ranking job overseeing personnel in the Washington police force. He had sat in the center of power and controversy during a turbulent time in the department and the city and had loved it. He had recruited hundreds of blacks and women onto what had been a largely white police force. The job brought him local fame and a sense of purpose and burnished his image as a hardworking, straight-arrow reformer who could reach out to the disadvantaged yet maneuver his way through the system.

In my mother, Michele, he had found a wife whom he also considered to be his best friend. She was widely acknowledged as brilliant and lively; he was proud of her growing reputation as a critic and poet. They presided over a bustling house filled with children and pets, books and music. The most important thing they shared might have been their love of writing. After he came home most nights, he would drop his briefcase, shed his blue suit, and disappear into a cloud of Tiparillo smoke in the den, where he would pound out experimental dramas about modern men and women grappling with moral dilemmas. One or two had been staged in the area and had won him the friendship and praise of some local artists. In his family, his job, and his writing, he balanced the contrasting sides of his personality.

A long time before my father had been the most wonderful man in the world. I had once sat on his lap every Saturday morning, clapping and waggling my feet, as he listened to his old records of Johnny Cash and Leadbelly and Mississippi John Hurt. On Sundays when I was small, he would plop me onto the back of his bicycle before pedaling up the street to buy the *New York Times*. Though my mother hated me to have too many sweets, he always stopped at the Esso station on the way home to buy me a Milky Way and an orange soda, risking her wrath to please me. Even at the age of four, moreover, I could tell he was important in the world. He drove an unmarked police car with a real siren in the glove compartment. He had been on television. My mother had once held a party in honor of one of his interviews and giddily shushed the guests when his face appeared on the screen.

But everything had changed after her brutal death from cancer in 1974. Around the same time, my father quit the police department for a more prosaic position at a federal agency. He fell out of the spotlight and lost the swagger that had accompanied his former job. He battled with his supervisor. Old colleagues lost track of him. Work had once been an arena in which he battled; now it was a vacuum into which he vanished.

The old newspaper articles about my father sat crumbling in forgotten scrapbooks buried in the bottom of bureau drawers. The family photo albums, meticulously kept by my mother, sat unopened in the bookcase. No one had added to them since her death.

Outside the office, he had struggled to build a personal life without my mother. But he often seemed unsure of what to do. In an effort to modernize himself, he traded in our faded gold Oldsmobile for a snappier, beige Volkswagen Rabbit. He discovered a hot new crepe restaurant in the city, where he could bring dates. He took up jogging—briefly. He suddenly went out one afternoon and bought new furniture for the living room. He bought two leisure suits to spiff up his ward-robe. One, I remember, was a vivid light blue, accessorized with a white belt and white shoes. It was Exhibit A in my private action accusing him of trying too hard.

On top of all this, he had a household to run by himself. Piles of unsorted laundry sat on chairs throughout the house, waiting for him. Dirty dishes stacked up in the sink. Almost every day one of us needed him to run out and get something at the grocery store.

While he was juggling all these challenges, the family over which he presided, minus the magnetizing presence of my mother, began to fly apart. My brother David, who was ten years older than me, was the first to go. He joined the merchant marines just six months after her death and spent the next few years waiting for ships in New Orleans or sailing the seas, returning only for occasional short visits. Jonathan, who was eighteen months younger than David, lived at home while attending college but was so occupied with classes and work most of the time that he was rarely around. When he was home, he quit eating meals with us or even sitting in the living room to watch television with us; though he didn't move out until after I entered high school, he usually stayed in his room, listening to Who records and plunking his guitar. My sister, Sarah, was thirteen when Mom died, with several years of high school to go. She felt the help she gave by cooking and cleaning was unappreciated by the rest of us, and she and I fell into increasingly frequent quarrels. She befriended another family down the street and spent more and more of her time with them, before leaving for college in the autumn of 1977 with palpable relief. Within a few years of my mother's death, my family of six had, for the most part, dwindled to a family of two: me and my father.

Amid all this drift, in the fall of 1978 Dad was unexpectedly offered a way to remake himself: an early retirement with partial benefits. His agency was being abolished, and all employees with enough tenure had the choice of leaving. Just fifty-two, he seized upon the opportunity as a lucky break and began to conjure up bold new plans. He would have more time to write, while perhaps earning easy extra money as a personnel consultant. Maybe he would get married again, or move us away from worn-out Washington. You could see him imagining that he had stumbled onto a hidden escape route from a dead end.

I too saw a chance to reinvigorate our lives. I felt like my father and I were leftovers from an old family and lobbied for a move to California or New England, distant places that held a romantic allure and promised a fresh start. He and I bought guidebooks and conspired over dinner.

One week the following spring, we even drove up to Massachusetts and Vermont to scout towns. We told ourselves one of them could be our new home. But we were strangely unsystematic about our explorations. We didn't look at houses or schools. We didn't meet any real estate agents or townspeople. We simply drove past elms and maples and across covered bridges, stopping when we felt like it, soaking up the scenery and then hitting the road again. By the third or fourth day we were driving aimlessly. Lofted by the excitement of possibility, we quietly lowered ourselves to earth with the unspoken realization that we weren't very serious about this. I was suddenly frightened by the possibility of leaving everything I knew behind. For his part, my father seemed most interested not in the prospect of moving up here but in the opportunity to visit a priory in Vermont. We drove back home and didn't talk about moving anymore.

By that fall, humbled as I started classes with all the people to whom I had bid good-bye the previous spring, I had come to see the whole futile excursion as a reflection of the entropy afflicting us. It was as if we were locked into lives that we couldn't break out of. As my sense of Dad's ineffectiveness grew, his stature eroded before my eyes like California coastline.

He remained a nice, kind man, one with whom I could pleasantly discuss TV or sports or, if he was able to extract it from me, what I was doing at school. He never lost his temper, rarely said no, and never punished me. My friends considered me lucky to have such an easygoing father. He was almost like a friend.

But he was a sad, strangely distant figure too, a man whose stasis kept him from reaching out to me or letting me below his surface. I was starting to think I might become an actor or a writer, ambitions I believed he couldn't understand. Even though we were together all the time, we were slowly becoming less intimate. I silently began plotting my own flight from this dying, depressing household, a flight that would be just for me. Upon graduation, I intended to go far away to college. I might return occasionally to see my father, but I saw no future in this husk of a family. My father was an anchor. I wanted to swim for the surface.

❈ ❈ ❈

But my father had plans of his own. On the first day after his retirement, he woke up and did something unexpected: He went to mass. The place was called Holy Cross. It was about a ten-minute drive from our house and apparently was the local Catholic parish. I don't think anyone in my family had ever heard of it. I doubt if any of us had even been to a church in the five years since my mother's death. As the youngest child, I had been inside a traditional Catholic church only a handful of times in my entire life.

At first we didn't pay any attention. When David and Sarah came home to visit that year, Dad's churchgoing didn't come up. Jonathan and I never talked about it either. I probably slept so late most days of that summer that I wasn't even aware my father was sneaking off every morning until a few months had passed. No one gave too much thought to what Dad did. When his churchgoing started to become a topic of conversation, it was as a joke. My friend Steve drew a big laugh the time he dubbed Dad "the Brother from Another Planet."

My father's newfound devotion gradually became more apparent. But even then it seemed less a transformation than just another phase testifying to his tiresome, tortuous struggle to fill up his life. It certainly didn't seem like a radical break from his past; indeed, in some ways it made perfect sense. He had always been a quiet, somewhat introspective person with a religious inclination. He wrestled with questions of God and faith in his reading and writing; his favorite author was Dostoyevsky. In his personnel work, he had shown an almost missionary zeal, especially toward poor and underprivileged applicants. He had always been a bit of a loner in our family, in which my brilliant, talkative, hyperactive mother had been the sun around which we orbited. Even the chores he preferred were solitary, like cutting the grass or getting down on his hands and knees to scrub the bathroom floors every weekend. One outlet for his spiritual side had been yoga: For a while, when I was small, I had grown used to stumbling downstairs in the darkness of an early morning to find the startling sight of my father standing on his head in the middle of the living room rug, gravity mischievously tugging his pajama top toward the floor.

He seemed always to be striving for some sort of spiritual equilibrium. Though he rarely sat down to have serious talks with his children and almost never hugged us or spoke of his emotions, he tried to be easygoing and friendly. Yet it took some effort, as if he were holding himself up to some standard; as my sister once said, while we could tell he loved us, it often seemed as if he would prefer to be off on a mountaintop somewhere. In a household in which all four children had inherited my mother's moodiness, he tended to be as even-tempered as a calm sea. It took an unusual event, such as the angry slam of a door, to trigger even a sharp word from him. When he did lose his temper, it was less intimidating than comical, with his raspy voice, red cheeks, and threats to "raise hell." He never held a grudge.

We'd always considered ourselves a Catholic family, though in practice we'd had what amounted to an extended dalliance with the church. Dad had been religious growing up, while Mom had converted from Judaism when she was twenty. During their marriage they fell in and out of the church, balancing periods of devotion with long stretches of absenteeism.

By the time my mother died, they had grown far from orthodox Catholicism. While my brothers and sister had sometimes been dragged to mass when they were small, the family hadn't attended a traditional neighborhood church since long before I was born. I had been given almost no exposure to the traditional tenets of the faith. We had occasionally said grace when my mother was alive, but without much reverence. Most of what I knew about Catholicism came from a decidedly unorthodox group of liberal Catholics that my parents had joined when I was three. In a fit of post–Vatican II euphoria, they gathered weekly in a high school auditorium in northern Virginia to read the Gospels and share communion, supplementing the service with winsome guitar music, excerpts from *Jonathan Livingston Seagull*, and even occasional interpretive dances.

My father's sudden immersion in the life of a suburban Catholic parish was thus notable, but it was not a true departure from his history. At least, for a long while, it didn't seem that way.

❧ ❧ ❧

The appearance of the prayer groups, though, was an early sign of the unprecedented fervor with which Dad was taking this new interest, as well as the incursions it would make into our daily routine. As the months passed, others became unavoidable.

Reluctantly, I took notice of the prayer manuals that began appearing on tables around the house, next to stacks of biographies of saints and thick books on Roman Catholic doctrine and theology. Dad would sit for hours balancing these volumes in his lap, using a pencil to scribble notes in the margins or on note cards in his squat, illegible handwriting. He lined the books along a shelf in the living room until they pushed some of the art books and cookbooks collected by my mother into other bookcases farther back in the house. Meanwhile, the rows of novels and plays that lined Mom's den and Dad's bedroom, collected by them together over decades, grew dusty.

He started carrying a set of rosary beads from room to room, along with the armful of objects he already toted about the house, which typically included at least one book, several pens and pencils, a small alarm clock, his reading glasses, and a small purse, which itself contained his checkbook, several packs of gum, and more pens and pencils.

He began to disappear to his den or his bedroom for stretches of an hour or more. I eventually figured out that he was going off to pray. My brother Jonathan called it "dialing long-distance," and that phrase became one form of family shorthand for Dad's new life. "Where's Dad?" someone would ask, and the answer would come: "Dialing long-distance."

At some point Dad hired a crew of workers to renovate our nearly abandoned basement. They cleaned up the jagged pieces of tile on the floor, laid down a thin, red carpet, and removed the nails that extended from the steps leading down. Dad moved his big white recliner and a small table down there and began using the space for private retreats. I learned to leave the door closed and walk softly when my father was downstairs. After an hour or two, I would hear him coming up the steps. Emerging into the light of the dining room, he seemed weary and slightly disoriented, like a deep-sea diver returning to the surface.

He launched a brief, mostly unsuccessful career as a missionary. Needy strangers were invited to board at our house, and my cooperation was solicited. One was a sad, very old man whose wife was undergoing surgery at a nearby hospital. Another was an old friend of my father's who was recovering from severe burns on her feet and calves. During her three-week stay, she commandeered the living room, where she chain-smoked, issued bossy opinions, and enlisted my father as her aide-de-camp. He drove her to doctor appointments, served her meals, and counseled her, sometimes even prodding her to return with him to the church. But weeks after she arrived, I came home one afternoon to find her sitting on our porch chattering in an incoherent and eerily shapeless stream of words. I tried to converse, but she kept shooting off on tangents of her own. As soon as I could excuse myself, I slipped upstairs.

There my brother Jonathan grabbed me by my shirt. "She's drunk," he whispered. He showed me where she had been filching drinks from a bottle of Scotch in his room. She had even consumed half a bottle of his aftershave and some mouthwash.

I had never seen an alcoholic before and found the experience deeply upsetting. My sympathy for her situation conflicted with my irritation at her behavior and the sense that my home kept being invaded by strangers. Just as bad, what I saw as my father's clearly fruitless efforts to influence her served to increase his impotence in my eyes. The lines between his private religious life and our home life kept blurring.

I finally went to him in the den and told him that, much as I wanted to support his new life, I did not want to be recruited as his volunteer. He seemed saddened by my complaint but said he understood. His friend moved out. After that, Dad kept his missionary experiments outside the house.

But of all the signs of change in my father, the most disturbing one was his tears.

I learned of these by accompanying him to mass. Confused by the conflicting messages of his new life, I sometimes experienced intermittent spells of virtue in the early months of his return to the church that tempted me to go with him. I hadn't yet lost all my childhood faith. Moreover, watching someone in our family attending regular Sunday services for the first time in my life, I saw the appeal in that weekly ritual of rising and gathering to worship. If the intensity of my father's devotion sometimes inhibited me, I rationalized: How far it could it really go, after all?

Holy Cross Church, the center of what I was coming to think of as my father's secret life, was a red-brick building that stood back from a busy road at the apex of a half-moon driveway. A school building jutted out uncomfortably to the left, like a third arm. To enter the church, you walked beneath an enormous, round, stained-glass window and through heavy wooden doors. The inside walls were painted a sickly institutional color somewhere between green and yellow. Wooden beams spanned the high ceiling. The building was freezing in the winter and steaming hot in the summer.

Most of the parishioners were elderly couples or harried young parents with squirmy, small children. The pastor had a crew cut and wore glasses with thick black frames. During mass, he droned on like an accountant at a tax seminar. He liked to begin his homilies with the words, "Imagine you're on a ship in outer space . . ." Several other priests in residence struck me as ancient reactionaries or embarrassing would-be hipsters in Hush Puppies who wanted to relate. The bland intonations of the lectors and the rote, mumbled prayers of the parishioners nearly lulled me to sleep. Down on my knees on the narrow little kneeler, I found praying, or even any feeling of reverence, all but impossible. The driving purpose of mass seemed to be to finish as quickly as possible so everyone could get home to watch the Redskins game. If God was anywhere, I quickly concluded, he was not at Holy Cross parish on Sunday morning.

Not that it mattered much to me anyway. Whatever good intentions had propelled me from my warm bed into the pew, I always ended up craning my neck over my shoulder to catch a glimpse of the clock on the back wall even before the service began.

And my discomfort only increased when my father started to cry. Every time I went, I hoped he wouldn't, but it was always the same scene. As soon as we walked in, found a pew, and sat down, my father shut his eyes. He acted as if I wasn't even there. Deep in concentration, he furrowed his brow. His face grew troubled and stiff as candle wax. Beneath closed eyelids, he seemed to be focusing intently on an obscure dot in the distance.

By the time we stood for the entrance hymn, he was almost grimacing in pain. I could feel myself shrinking in importance as mass began. He seemed marooned. If I leaned over to say something, he glared at me and returned to his meditation. I learned to just leave him alone.

After a few minutes, little canals of salty tears began running down his cheeks. They dribbled around his chin and into the creases in his neck. He ignored them. His mustache became saturated and his face glistened with moisture. Bubbles of snot popped in his nostrils.

I knew that everyone around us would begin to sneak glances at him. I could feel their eyeballs on the back of my neck. I sensed that once mass ended the other families went home and talked about the man who always cried at mass. No one ever said anything to me. But inside, I shriveled in humiliation at the spectacle that was my father.

Then, just when he seemed about to break down completely, he pulled a crumpled, dirty handkerchief from his back pocket and ran it across his face, in one gesture wiping off all the accumulated gunk and blowing his nose with a loud snuffle. I hoped this might signal the end of his outburst, but the tears kept coming. We stood and knelt and stood and knelt and walked up the aisle for communion, and the tears kept coming. We returned to our seats and sat twitching as we waited for the priest to dismiss us, and the tears kept coming. The priest delivered a final prayer and the organist played one last song and around us people zipped up their coats and children fidgeted, and the tears kept coming. Hours seemed to pass, and the tears kept coming.

By the end of the service, Dad was thoroughly lost. His frame was bent, his face wet and red. Gingerly I would reach through the fog and tap him on the shoulder. Without saying a word or even looking my way, he would put his hand into his jacket pocket. The hand seemed to have broken away from his body and begun acting of its own free will. It fished around, excavated the car keys, and held them out in my direction. I grabbed them and raced out of the suffocating building. In the front passenger seat of the car, I would turn up the radio and wait. Five or ten minutes later he would appear, and we would drive home in silence.

I soon quit church altogether. But as my interest waned, his intensified. Two years after his return, he was living the life of a suburban mendicant. He spent hours at the church each morning. He had quit consulting and stopped dating. He had burned his plays and given up writing. He had stopped going to movies. He had quit reading fiction, even his detective novels, and now read only obscure, church-related books with off-putting titles like *The Spirit Within*. He prayed for hours a day. His demeanor had changed: He was humbler, worn-looking, quieter. He gave up desserts, restricted his diet to simple foods, and some nights even skipped dinner.

He seemed to have deliberately reduced his horizons to the church at Holy Cross and our own four walls. When he wasn't at church, or out with a friend from church, he was home almost all the time. I felt crowded by his presence. I had spent the years between my mother's death and his retirement roaming about the house more or less freely in the afternoons. Now I tripped over him constantly. He dropped me off at school in the morning and was waiting on the couch when I arrived home in the afternoon to ask me about my day. He stayed there to watch *General Hospital* with me. Just as I was discovering what a burden he was, he seemed to be trying to become my buddy.

I began to wonder whether he wasn't reaching out to me as some sort of religious obligation. He never proselytized or prodded me to go back to mass once I stopped. But I noticed that he had begun to go at his household duties, most of which revolved around my needs, with an abject humility and seriousness that seemed inspired by more than a simple desire to be a good parent. He leapt up to do the dishes. He embraced the laundry. He made me whatever I wanted for dinner. This was somewhat uncharacteristic; as a father, he had never before been too interested in my life. Was he doing all this because he loved me, I wondered, or because he loved God?

In response, I resolved to mete out my affection in small doses. I wasn't about to reject his services, of course. But with a stubborn and silent coldness, I decided that I would withhold from him any signs that could be misconstrued as approval of his new religious life. Once I was gone, he could do as he pleased. Until then, I wanted a father, not a prophet.

One November day when I was sixteen, my father asked me to sit down at our dining room table and have a talk with him.

This was an unappealing invitation. By my count, it would be only the second or third serious talk I had ever had with my father. Though he was well-meaning and thoughtful, I'd never found him to be as good at giving advice as the fathers on television were. Once when I was about nine, I had asked him for advice in winning the heart of a girl I had a crush on. After pondering the question, he very thoughtfully and deliberately suggested I comb my hair and keep my fingernails clean. I had not been back for a follow-up. When I learned about sex, it was from my best friend, Steve, who passed the information on the day after he heard it from his father. I thought he was making it up.

By this time, my father and I were together much of the day, of course, but neither of us shared many details about our inner lives. Deep into my moody adolescence, I privately dreamt of flight while cultivating a studied indifference to the world at large and, particularly, to him. He shared stories and gossip about his church friends but was too smart to try to engage me in a serious discussion about faith. Our interactions amounted to little more than a steady stream of chatter about the surface events of our days, the news, television, and family gossip.

Now my father sat across from me, arms on the table, expression serious, as I slouched in my seat. He was clearly nervous.

His life had been changing, he said.

As I knew, he had become very religious. He felt God was calling him elsewhere. He didn't know where yet. Maybe to the priesthood. Maybe to some sort of social mission. He just didn't know, and he wasn't sure when he would.

But he had made some decisions about simplifying his life. He wanted to cut back.

So he would be selling our house this year. We would move into an apartment. He thought he would probably sell or give away a lot of our furniture and books. I might want to think about what things I wanted to keep.

He felt sure his future would be intimately involved with the Lord. He and his spiritual advisor, a priest in Canada, were trying to figure out what he should do. Maybe he would stay in Washington, but he had doubts. Things were liable to change, radically.

He loved me. He intended to ensure that I was settled at college before he made any drastic moves. He would be there for me. He would not let me go to college without being financially protected. If I had any concerns, he wanted to hear them. He wanted to stay in my life. But he just didn't see himself sitting around an empty house for the rest of his life and waiting for his grandchildren to visit him once a year. God was calling him someplace else.

He was happy. He was peaceful. He didn't even feel that he was making the decisions in his life anymore. God was.

Did I have any questions?

As I listened with an impassive expression, my mind seemed simultaneously to speed up and slow down. Given the way his life had been heading, I was not completely surprised. Then again, I was stunned to hear the official end of the family declared so casually. A rush of conflicting emotions welled up inside me: I wanted him to be happy, but I wanted him to be unhappy, too. I wanted him to remain there for me, but I wanted to leave. I wanted to be selfish, and I wanted to be generous. I was sixteen and did not want him to think that anything he did was in any way going to affect my own life. I knew everything was going to change but could not envision the concrete ways in which my father's new life was going to affect my own.

All at once, too, I understood that the creeping feeling I had possessed for years of a family slowly deteriorating around me like an old house, as my mother died and my brothers and sister left home and I grew up and my father grew old, was being confirmed by my father. He knew it too, and in a strange way realizing that made me feel closer to him. Neither his future nor mine lay within these walls. Instead of just me, both of us would be leaving all this. Not imminently, but soon enough.

What could I ask? I didn't know if I wanted him to change his mind, didn't think he wanted to or that I could make him change it anyway. I could not begin to understand what religious impulse he felt, but I knew it was a strong one. I didn't want to just sit there and feign interest while he went on about his devotion to Christ.

I simply shrugged. I told him I had nothing to ask. I mumbled some thanks to him for talking to me about it. Then I quickly rose and walked away from the table, relieved that this awkward talk was over.

But with every step I took away from him, an unsettling thought ran through my head like an electric current: Either God himself has stormed into my father's life and shaken it to the roots for reasons I can't fathom, or my father has finally gone crazy.

Two

✦ ✦ ✦

When he reached his late sixties, my father once told me, he began to be visited by overwhelming images from his past. They sprang up suddenly, when he was at the sink brushing his teeth or sitting at breakfast reading a magazine in the near-total darkness of an early morning. His head would be flooded with memories of a long-ago argument with my mother, a nasty political battle at work, or a harrowing encounter with his father. There seemed no clear pattern to the recollections, but he was struck that most touched on some minor failure of his. They were as mysterious as question marks and suggestively tapped deeper recesses of emotion or memory than the immediate episodes recalled. They often evoked hints of the larger historical events he had lived through, such as the Depression of his childhood or the civil rights marches he witnessed from his office window in Washington. In a flash, a memory might remind him of some of the many people he had known—his wife, his mother, his brothers, his college friends—whose lives and fates would be laid out before him. All rushed by as if carried

by a great river. With no warning, a memory would swell,
stagger him briefly, then dissipate.

He did not attach much importance to these images,
though some of them were painful. Vivid pictures had always
filled his head, from the rich dreams that brightened his
sleep to the imaginary faces and people he had been con-
juring since childhood. But he did find, when reliving these
moments, that he viewed them in a new light. He could look
straight at his shortcomings without flinching. Events that
once seemed to be great mysteries or dead ends fell into place
as signposts on a journey.

What they suggested to him, he felt, was a life unified by
the cleansing power of prayer. He did not, by this time, know
of any part of his internal life that was not connected with
that ancient practice. Indeed, just as he entered old age he
had reshaped his days around it. He had traveled a long way
from being the frustrated suburban homeowner and government retiree who, nearly fifteen years earlier, had tried to
share a glimpse of his soul with the sullen teenaged boy staring at him from across the dining room table. He had taken
a long, sometimes dark journey toward nothing less than the
center of meaning.

In 1982, the year after he told me of his plans, my father
sold our house and got rid of most of our possessions. For
the next eighteen months he kept an apartment. I was with
him for the first nine of those months, but the year after I left
to attend college in Chicago he gave up the apartment, too.
He kept only a few religious books, some shirts, pants, and underwear, and his toiletries. These possessions were not quite

enough to fill two suitcases. He carefully placed his bags in the backseat of the car and launched himself into the world.

He was living almost by instinct now, trying to go where his prayer life seemed to be leading him. He was more than four years into his religious journey, and it still did not make full sense to him. He thought of himself as a toddler taking his first steps.

For nearly a year he lived like a pilgrim, staying with different sets of friends and relatives while he tried to discern the nature of his calling. He wrote seeking advice from priests and monks he knew. In long letters to friends, he poured out his doubts and questions yet reaffirmed his faith in Christ. He prayed for hours each day and waited for a sign. He researched monasteries that welcomed older candidates and visited one or two. He wondered whether he should become a parish priest and made some inquiries. Nothing, for months, bore fruit.

Though he maintained confidence in God's plan for him, he sometimes wrestled with doubts about what he had done. Most stemmed from the frayed state of the family. He was sure his children didn't understand what he was doing. The five family members had scattered across the country and were barely in touch with one another.

Finally, the Canadian priest who was giving him spiritual guidance advised him to let go. "The Lord wants you to keep letting your children know that they have a home, a permanent home, within your very spirit," he wrote. But, he added, "your vocation now is much, much larger than your family, and it is urgent that you make your decisions in light of that larger vocation with the same abandonment that you have chosen so wholeheartedly up to now. The Lord's word is 'Do not be anxious about everything . . . you have a Father in heaven who knows you need all these things.'" The words liberated and lifted my father's heart.

By the middle of 1984, he believed he was being called to the priesthood. A priest he knew suggested he might make a good monk, too, and gave him the name of a small Benedictine monastery in central Illinois. After my father wrote to the place, the abbot invited him for a visit but tried to dampen any expectation my father might have about becoming a priest at his age.

Despite that discouragement, my father, with little else to do, decided to drive to the Midwest for an eight-day visit that September. The monastery, Saint Bede Abbey, was located in Peru, Illinois, a small town about a hundred miles southwest of Chicago. He arrived in the middle of a hot afternoon and met a round, middle-aged monk in a dark robe, who led him down a dark corridor to a guest room on the first floor. When that door opened, my father was struck by a burst of light and an overwhelming sense of peace. He knew this was where he was meant to be.

The monks seemed to respond to his presence, too. They invited him back for a month the following spring. He returned in March and never left again. Seven years later, he took vows of stability, conversion through a monastic way of life, and obedience and became a member of the community of Saint Bede Abbey for life. The following year, now in his midsixties, he knelt before a bishop and received ordination as a Roman Catholic priest.

To most people in my father's life, he is now known simply as Father James. He lives with about thirty other men, most of them middle-aged or older. He provides spiritual counsel to several dozen people from the area and works with the sick and dying at a nearby hospital. He presides at Sunday masses in the area and sometimes at daily mass at the monastery.

Still handsome, with a gray beard, thinning hair, and a broad smile, he is a vigorous man, friendly and open, with an infectious laugh. But he remains a bit of a loner, happiest by himself in prayer. Three times a day he joins his brothers in group prayers derived from the Psalms. On his own he prays for hours more.

In his seventies, my father is fulfilled, a man finally at home with his past and himself. He loves his life. He lives as a witness to the truth of Christ.

Yet to me he is a mystery. A part of his heart remains hidden.

What happened to my father? What does it mean?

❖ ❖ ❖

Fittingly, I was starting to ask such questions at the same time my father was recalling his own past. They were questions I had not bothered to ask for a long time. For years, it was enough to know that he had left us. I did not need to know why.

Where he saw the story of a long, personal journey toward God, I saw one of a retreat from the world that I could not fathom. During my college years and the subsequent period,

I watched him from afar and wavered in my feelings. Sometimes I couldn't help but admire his determination to find his way in uncharted territory. Other times I resented him. I could not understand why he had broken up our lives and gone to live in seclusion.

My mixed feelings about his situation were complicated by larger questions of meaning. Like many people in their early twenties, I had little faith, many questions, and scant motive to live a Christian life. It wasn't that I didn't believe in God, exactly; it was more that I knew that either a yes or a no answer carried implications I was not prepared to act on. I fell far away from the church, as much out of inertia as deliberation.

My muddled thoughts about religion made it hard to know what to think of my father's situation. I did not consider myself a believer. My father was living a life that baffled me. The very idea of joining a religious community was completely outside my experience. But from my doubts I could not leap to the conclusion that my father was following a fruitless path. I knew he saw a purpose, even if I could not fathom what it was. Deep down, moreover, I felt an impalpable love for him that I could not shake. It was a love I was often loath to admit or address, but one that clung adamantly to my heart and refused to be forgotten, no matter how hard I tried.

And so I concluded that it was best to leave the whole tangle and proceed with my life. At some point, I decided, I'll know what to think. For the time being, I looked back on our talk at the dining room table as the site of an amicable parting. My father had searched until he had found a path for himself. I had to do the same. I tried to become a bystander as our family dismantled itself like a house at auction.

In the months following our talk, my father swept up our lives as if impelled by a force outside himself. He was showing more energy and determination than he had displayed in years. Six months before my high school graduation, he sold our house. Over one weekend in midwinter we sorted through our possessions and pared them down to the essentials. Chairs, couches, lamps, tables, toys, utensils, trivets, pottery, books, paintings, rugs, place mats, candlesticks, magazine racks, toys, and bookends were sold or given away at a two-day yard sale. Someone bought the art book whose spine I had seen on our shelf every day of my life. Someone else walked off with the spotted stuffed dog that had been my favorite childhood companion. Everything vanished into the trunks and backseats of strangers. Seated on the lawn in a metal chair, I watched as my father, the impresario of the sale, scurried about. He obviously felt that the process of getting rid of our possessions was little more than a time-consuming chore that had to be completed so he could proceed. He seemed almost happy to let go of the detritus of a lifetime. It was only one of many times during those months that I was struck by the sheer joy he seemed to feel in uprooting his life. Of course, he was uprooting mine as well, but having determined to adopt an indifferent face, I could not let him see how hard it was to leave our old lives behind. It wouldn't have changed what was happening, anyway.

We packed the things we were keeping into boxes. One weekend we rented a truck and moved into a two-bedroom apartment several miles away. This would be a temporary home, for me, him, and my sister, Sarah, who had moved back with us briefly before leaving for graduate school.

Our new apartment was on the second floor of an anonymous red-brick building in a development of tennis courts, cul-de-sacs, swinging singles, and retirees. Months after we moved in, I still got lost driving home along the winding streets, trying to pick out the right building. My sister claimed the back bedroom, and I got the narrow one near the living room. Dad slept on the couch. By the time we had settled in, I already had been accepted at college. I treated the place as if I were a short-term boarder.

That spring I graduated from high school, and my father took us out to dinner. The following autumn he drove me out to Chicago and dropped me off at school. I flew home once more, at Christmas, when we sifted through the remaining belongings. David, who had settled in St. Louis and planned to attend college, got most of my parents' paintings and the dishes. Jonathan, now living in New York, took some of the books and records. Sarah, who had made plans to move to California, claimed the rest.

Offered anything I wanted, I asked only for the family photo albums, the old scrapbooks of articles, and my mother's sewing kit, which I thought I might need. I told everyone that since I probably would be moving frequently over the next few years, I didn't want to be weighed down by a lot of old stuff. When I got back to campus, the albums and scrapbooks went into the bottom of a battered old cardboard box in the basement. The sewing kit was shoved into the back of the closet.

For several years after that holiday, our family was in touch only occasionally. After my father gave up the apartment the following spring, the threads that bound us grew as thin as the silvery strands of a spider web. Weeks passed without a phone call between me and my father. During the months when he moved from friend to friend and drove around the countryside visiting monasteries, I didn't often know what he was doing. When he did call, I rarely thought to ask him where he was. Today, when I hear him recall that time, I'm amazed at how little I knew of his travels, of the people with whom he stayed, of his day-to-day life.

I was wrapped up in studies, making new friends and inventing a new life for myself. I had decided to become a writer, and to nurture for myself an image as a rootless and independent outsider. It was neither a realistic nor a successful effort, but it justified my decision to keep my father at a distance. With Dad in seclusion, I told myself my life was like a clean blackboard unburdened by the past.

Yet I was always a little envious when my friend Bob's mother arrived for weekly visits with loads of clean laundry, bags of groceries, and words of admonition. Where was my parent? Some friends phoned their parents regularly, hosted their brothers and sisters, went home for weekends. I could go months without talking to anyone in my family at all.

Before school vacations, I waved good-bye to my friends, then rented a temporary room in a fraternity house or student flat. Once when I could find no place to stay before the dorms reopened, a friend snuck me into a back room in one of the school cafeterias. I hid away there, surrounded by boxes and suitcases, for two weeks.

The first Christmas I spent on my own, I stayed in the apartment of friends who needed someone to tend to their parakeet while they were away over the break. With its owners absent, the bird immediately became hysterical, scrunching into a ball, squeezing through its bars, and flying wildly around the apartment, banging into walls and perching in remote corners of the ceiling to squawk. For days it refused to eat. I knew how unsettled it felt.

On a bitter-cold Christmas Eve, I worked all day fixing sandwiches at my restaurant job, then carried a sandwich and soda home for a weirdly subdued Christmas Eve meal while the bird dive-bombed my scalp. I slept in the next morning, watched a little TV, then went to a friend's house for dinner. No one in my family called me, and I didn't call any of them. I wasn't sad, exactly, since it was partly by my choice. But it felt strange to be without my family. It was a little mystifying that none of us seemed to want to be together. What had led us here? I wondered that all Christmas Day. I came home to an empty apartment to find the parakeet dead on the floor, spent, I guessed, from all the flapping and mental anguish.

Still, I determined to keep setting my own course. That winter I took a semester off from school, loaded a backpack, and flew to Europe. In early January I arrived in Luxembourg—though not exactly my idea of a European paradise, it had been the cheapest destination—and figured out how to use the bus to get to the inexpensive hotel I had read about in my dog-eared copy of *Let's Go Europe*. I rode a train to Milan, where I sat on the hard, wooden pews of the bombastic, airy train station one frigid night after frost on the train tracks had halted all traffic, chatting with an English cabinetmaker while I waited for the exchange to open at eight o'clock so I could get some lire. The next morning I got a room and slept the sweetest sleep of my life for seventeen hours straight, reflecting as I nodded off that no one, anywhere, knew where I was. In Paris I bought myself a pair of big black boots and strutted about. I started to grow a wispy beard and congratulated myself on my ability to order alcohol in public places. I checked into a freezing, five-dollar-a-night hotel crammed with other traveling students and fantasized about my sexual initiation. While dreaming, I completely missed the suggestive hints dropped by my roommate, a sophomore from Oberlin, whom I later heard leaving her bed in the middle of the night to rendezvous with the guy upstairs. In a real French restaurant, I acceded when the waitress recommended that I order a salad topped with something she called "moozeau." Not until I had gobbled down all the strange sliced meat on top could I convince her to explain what the word meant: snout.

When I ran short of funds three weeks sooner than expected, I spent all but my last dollar on a bus ticket to the Luxembourg airport, only to arrive on a cold evening after it had closed. I sat up on my backpack in the cold outside the locked front door, shivering and singing "99 Bottles of Beer" over and over to stay awake, until at three o'clock the parking-lot attendant took pity on me and let me sleep on one of the orange plastic chairs inside. The next day I flew home, carrying exactly enough money to pay for a subway ride from the Chicago airport back to my old dorm.

During my entire odyssey abroad, it never once occurred to me to call my father.

❊   ❊   ❊

But one day that spring, he called me. I was clean-shaven again and living in an apartment off-campus. Dad said he was on his way to a monastery near Chicago and wanted to come visit.

I offered him the sofa while I slept in a sleeping bag on the floor. Neither of us had much money, so we ate in. I told him about my life at school and introduced him to some of my friends. We went for a lot of walks. One day he went out on his own, found the local Catholic church as if by radar, and came home to brief me on everything he'd learned about the priest and parish. But Dad didn't tell me much about his new life, and I didn't ask, though he did seem excited by the possibility that this monastery might be the place for him. He told me he would know more after a month.

A few weeks later he called to tell me he was staying indefinitely. Suddenly, unexpectedly, my father was back in my life—sort of—living less than two hours away. He was easy to reach, too: Once he settled in, he gave me his car.

But inertia is hard to overcome. I moved toward him slowly, tentatively. He was by now far enough removed from my daily thoughts that it didn't often occur to me that he was close by. Even when I did think of driving down there, I was sure I'd be uncomfortable seeing him at the abbey, wearing one of those robes and living with all these strange men. It would be less like a family reunion than a step back into the Middle Ages. I didn't know how often he was permitted to speak or whether I would even be welcomed by the other monks. I knew that they considered him part of their family now.

We did talk on the telephone more often, now that he had a regular phone number. He invited me to call him anytime I needed to, day or night. But reaching him at the abbey could be a maddening experience. The monks kept only one phone, in the front lobby. Some old man would answer it in a quiet, hollow voice, "Saaaaint Bee-eede," sounding as if he were about to keel over at any minute. I would ask to speak to Brother James, as my father was known before he became a priest, then wait for several minutes, imagining a gnomelike figure in a robe shuffling through the dark, silent hallways of the monastery in search of my father.

About six months after he moved there, I finally accepted an invitation to drive down one Saturday. I arrived in mid-afternoon. Dad met me at the abbey's front door, wearing the dreaded robe and sandals with black socks. He gave me a quick tour, the way a college student eagerly shows his parents around campus on parents' weekend. He showed me the refectory, where he joined the monks for meals three times a day, a long, cavernous room with dark tiles on the floor and wooden tables where they clustered, eight to a group. Through a swinging door was an enormous kitchen, then staffed by a group of Carmelite nuns who chattered in Spanish. We snatched some cookies from the baking trays and poured cups of coffee from an urn that was refreshed every few hours. Out back was a small apple orchard, where he worked during the spring and summer afternoons, and beyond that several hundred acres of woods, whose paths he roamed as often as possible. Across the lawn was a modern-looking building, all sharp angles and bright red brick, which had been built in the seventies: the worship-assembly building. Downstairs was the main chapel, where mass was held every afternoon at five. Up a narrow staircase was the room where the monks met for daily prayers.

For a century, things here had run in a continuous stream. The life evolved with the church—the use of the vernacular had grown, the format of mass had changed—but the accent was on stability and consistency. My father was just the latest man to take a part in their community.

Not without some pique, I was struck by how much he seemed at home, at least far more in his element than the thinning pilgrim whom I had watched getting worn down in our old house. He was bubbling with plans—he was to go away to college, he was to learn Latin, he felt certain he was to become a priest. But I stayed only a few hours and didn't stick around for dinner. I told him I had to get back.

I returned a few months later with my friend Steve, who was visiting me from college in Indiana. Steve was much more convinced than I that my father had truly cracked up, but as we drove away that afternoon he told me he thought Dad had found the place where he belonged.

Over the next few years, I established a pattern, talking to Dad every week or two on the phone, driving down to see him once or twice a year. I got to know a few of the monks by name. Once he was settled, he began to spend a few days of his vacation with me every summer. He began to tell me about his life, his classes, his friends, his faith. With more tolerance than I had once shown, I listened.

From far away, we inched closer to each other. In his new role as a man of God, he began sending friends and family cards at every holiday. Usually he simply dashed off a religious message and signed his name. "Dear Matt," he wrote me one Easter. "'. . . the winter is past, the rains are over and gone. The flowers appear on the earth, the time of pruning the vines has come, and the song of the dove is heard in our land.' Love, Dad." This sort of thing was touching, if impersonal.

But two or three times he took the unusual step of opening his heart and writing to me in words I had never heard from him. He apologized for his failings as a father. He said he was sorry that he had not always been there when I was young and that he felt bad for breaking up the family. He could tell from a distance, too, that I was finding life after college harder than I expected, that my dreams of success and romance were not springing instantly to life as I had planned. He mined his own youth, about which I realized I knew next to nothing, to offer me guidance in mine.

"When I was your age, I had cut myself off from my family and was living in New York City trying to make a life," he once wrote. "I was very lonely. You are better off in almost every way than I was at the time. It all hinges, my son, on you not turning against yourself, on your being steady, and daring to move toward maximum fulfillment."

Several years into his life as a monk, he started to become interested again in the outside world. I discovered for the first time that he was a movie fanatic. During his visits, we rented two or three videos a day, films that I thought he would like but that he had been unable to see at the monastery. He was intensely interested in many of them and sometimes spoke to me about the movies he had watched as a boy. I found I wanted his approval of my taste. I bought him some compact discs of the old music that he had once loved. As we listened together, he closed his eyes and rocked as he always had, and I rediscovered the tunes I had listened to on his lap. We watched basketball games together and talked about politics. We went to mass—and, strangely, he no longer cried every time. He still owned and wore the same cotton shirts he'd brought with him from our house to the abbey all those years ago. He still carried them in the same suitcases he'd had since I was small.

Sometimes, if I imagined hard enough, it almost felt like nothing had changed.

※ ※ ※

On New Year's Day of 1992 my family reunited beneath the expansive ceilings of the chapel at Saint Bede. It was only the third time we'd been together in a decade. Those two occasions had been for the weddings of my brothers, and like them, this was a sacred event: My father, after years as junior monk, was taking his final vows as a monk of Saint Bede. They would affirm a lifelong commitment to his new community.

The chapel at Saint Bede is surprisingly sleek and modern. Skylights over the front ceiling fill the wide room with light, even on the short, grayish days of an Illinois winter. The walls stretch high up, dwarfing you in whiteness. The sanctuary has a red-brick floor, a massive but plain white altar that requires six men to lift it, and a simple metal cross on a stand that is placed almost surreptitiously at the back. Around its edges are rows of soft chairs where the monks and priests of Saint Bede sit at their daily celebration of mass.

By contrast, congregants sit in stiff, uncomfortable, white plastic chairs. They serve as a reminder that this is not a parish church. A few locals attend mass here, to be sure. But this room is arranged for the comfort of the men who live here, not the civilians who choose to worship here. The attitude toward them is cordial but slightly distant. Those who do not belong to Saint Bede are unquestionably visitors.

Though I had by now grown used to thinking of my father as a monk, I was a bit nervous that day. I knew he was happy in his new life and doing what was right for him, but to me his faith remained as abstract as a phantom. On this day signs of it were evident everywhere. Friends who had prayed with him trickled in and took their seats, while the monks hung banners and straightened chairs. The abbot was wearing a colorful formal gown and a towering miter on his head. The seriousness of the occasion moved but also unnerved me. From my seat at the front, I joked uneasily with my brother Jonathan and his wife, Liz, while we waited for the service to begin. Sarah, who was videotaping the ceremony for posterity, strutted about checking camera angles and plugging in cords like a miniature Cecil B. DeMille. We all kept looking toward the door for David and his wife, Germaine, who were late. We agreed that it was just like David to be late for something like this.

As the last guests sat down, Brother Mark, a stern-looking, middle-aged monk with a full beard and glasses, sat at the piano, then struck up the opening chords of a song. Programs in hand, we stood and sang:

> *O holy Mother, you brought to birth*
> *The King who reigns over heaven and earth*
> *For numberless days!*
> *With you we sing praise!*

Up the center aisle a procession moved past us: an incense bearer, two altar boys, and then, striding alone, my black-robed father. His head was bowed and his frame stiff as he reached the altar. Marching in twos, the monks of Saint Bede followed, the priests dressed in white, the brothers in black.

As we sat, the abbot, a tall man with round glasses and a flat speaking voice, sat in his throne by the altar. "Today, of course, is the day for resolutions," he told us. "However, we are to witness today more than a New Year's resolution. We are celebrating and witnessing someone making a vow for life, committing himself to the Lord in a type of life, a monastic way of life."

Now he summoned my father to his new life, singing in a quavering voice: "Come my son, listen to me."

Encircling him, the monks responded, "I will teach you the ways of the Lord." The words were a paraphrase of Psalm 34.

Dad stood with the posture of a schoolboy and walked to the abbot in the center of the sanctuary. He sat in a chair facing the abbot but below him, turning his back to us at an angle. I looked straight at the profile of my father's face.

The abbot spoke directly to him. "As you make your promises today toward that altar, and write and sign this document of your vows, that isn't it. That isn't going to be the end of it all. That's just the beginning.

"Our vows are promises of things that we can keep renewing in our lives, so that we will constantly be trying to grow and to increase in this love and seeking God. Your profession presumes you are imperfect." Dad smiled. "It presumes that you are making a commitment to seek God, and to grow in perfection, a promise that you are on a constant journey of seeking God, a journey that will not end, will not be completed, until you die. A monk fails in his vows when he stops seeking God, when he stops growing in the love of God and others.

"James, your job with the government was your career, but it was different from your marriage. Your marriage was your vocation, your calling. Now your vocation is to Saint Bede Abbey. It doesn't necessarily mean personal fulfillment, which no doubt will be there. It is an answer to God's call. Today you are solemnly consecrating your freedom and giving it to the Lord. Today he is to be your treasure."

The expression on my father's face was utterly serious, serene, a million miles away. He seemed to have been swallowed up by some huge thing that was entirely mysterious to me. He was only twenty yards from me, but he seemed farther away than he ever had before.

"For five years now, you have been pondering and praying, and so have we," the abbot told my father. "And you have decided, and so have we, that as far as we can tell God has called you to follow Christ in this monastic way of life. Brother James, I accept you for solemn profession."

"We also accept him," the monks echoed in stilted tones. "Thanks be to God." Everyone applauded as Dad shyly bobbed his head around the half-circle, an actor making a reluctant curtain call.

Now the abbot asked a few rote questions. Dad answered in a thin voice.

"Are you resolved to unite yourself more closely with Christ through the vows of solemn profession?"

"I am so resolved."

"Are you resolved with the help of God's grace to undertake that life of perfect chastity, obedience, and poverty which Christ our Lord and his Virgin Mother chose for themselves, and persevere in it forever?"

"I am so resolved."

With those words, I thought the ceremony might be just about over. But now came the most unexpected part of the day: My father stood, turned toward the altar, and lay down on his stomach, straight as an arrow pointed at the cross, his legs together, his face resting on his arms, shielded from view.

Unexpectedly, I was awed. Prostrate before the cross, humbled, Dad suddenly seemed like the only man I had ever known who had followed his beliefs to their limits.

Now the monks joined their voices in the Litany of the Saints, their song sounding like the voices of ancient people reaching to us through centuries. I watched my father, still on the floor, and the music began to carry me away:

> *Holy Mary, Mother of God . . . pray for us!*
> *Holy angels of God . . . pray for us!*
> *Saint John the Baptist . . . pray for us!*
> *Saint Joseph . . . pray for us!*
> *Saint Peter and Saint Paul . . . pray for us! . . .*

For ten timeless minutes, the invocations continued. When they finished, I felt refreshed.

As the monks returned to their seats, Dad rose, then got down on one knee before the abbot. The abbot handed him a scroll, and he read aloud the words he'd committed to paper earlier in the day. They were the actual vows.

"In the name of our Lord Jesus Christ, amen. I, Brother James Michael Murray, of Bethesda, Maryland, Archdiocese of Washington, D.C., promise with solemn vows before God and His saints, in the presence of our father in Christ Abbot Roger Corpus and the monks of this monastery, stability in this community, conversion through a monastic way of life, and obedience according to the rule of our holy father, Benedict, and the law proper to our congregation. In witness whereof I have prepared this document and signed it here at Saint Bede, in the year of our Lord 1992, on the first day of January, the feast of the solemnity of Mary, Mother of God."

He rose, strode to the altar, and signed the document. Turning back to the abbot, he extended his arms and petitioned God three times:

"Support me, Lord, as you have promised, that I may live, and do not disappoint me in my hope."

The abbot blessed him, then placed around his neck a cuculla, a black hooded choir robe that made my father look like a warlock. As we sang, "Where charity and hope are found, there is God," his back facing us, the monks left their seats and lined up slowly, and one by one, each came to my father and embraced him. I could not turn away from this receiving line.

Finally, it was finished. Dad removed the cuculla, then shuffled back to his seat, alone. He picked his program up off the chair, looked for the right page, and sat down. He might have been someone at the theater, returning from intermission. He seemed small and human again, in a comforting way. After the drama of the ceremony, he was my father again. For the first time that day, I relaxed.

Like the other monks, Dad closed his eyes to pray as the Eucharist was prepared. Everyone watched him. Not until the abbot spoke again, and most people had turned their attention away from my father, did he remove his glasses and wipe his eyes with his handkerchief.

From my seat, I watched with my brothers and sister as my father joined his new family, saw the tranquillity and purpose in his eyes, and began to wonder about the old family. For years now, I had heard a lot of theories from friends about why my father was a monk. Most, at first, didn't know what to make of it. Then they would bombard me with questions: Is that Catholic? Can he talk? Are you allowed to see him? Was he always religious? Is he celibate? How could he do that to himself?

Then came the cheap explanations: He was lonely. He was deluded. He was fleeing the world. He had had a breakdown. He missed my mother. Some people seemed to think that becoming a monk was simply a nice thing to do. I think they imagined a monastery as a type of elaborate retirement home, where the elderly could dress in loose-fitting clothing and spend their days occupied with activities like praying and gardening and crafts.

But none of these explanations had ever satisfied me, and now as I watched my father taking his final vows of commitment to his brothers, I understood why. Whatever may have happened, my father had an almost bottomless conviction. Despite what some people thought, despite my own doubts, he had not chosen an easy life. He was living a mentally intense life. He was working harder than he ever had before, often with people who were dying and despairing, and he was spending more time alone. Yet he was invigorated. If I was still reluctant to embrace his belief myself, I wasn't ready to dismiss the possibility that God had called my father to this new life. I could see in Dad's bearing, his manner, his eyes, that something had happened that wasn't easy to explain.

In a way I envied him. In my late twenties, I had reached a point where I was trying to reconcile life as it is lived with life as I had imagined it would be. As a writer, I was something less than the smash I had expected to be. I had held a series of short-term, low-paying newspaper jobs filled with plenty of drudgery and little glamour. I was distressed by my own laziness and lack of inspiration. I was letting go of old friends, spending too much time in front of the TV, piling up debts. Sometimes I wondered whether I believed in God, but I toyed with the idea of God's existence like a child poking at embers with a stick. In fifteen years, it seemed my father and I had traded places. He had once been lost in a quicksand of crisis, while I raced ahead with a plan and a destination. Now he was settled and happy, while I was sputtering. I was full of questions; he had found an answer.

That was the day I started to think more consciously about his life and try to unravel what had happened to him. In the months that followed, I started to ask him questions about his childhood and his beliefs. I asked him how he filled his days at the monastery, and whether he had always believed in God. I asked him what he thought happened when we died, and what had changed in his life back in 1979. At some point, I started writing down his answers.

One day I went down to the basement and dug out the old family photographs. I pulled the large portraits out of the books, took them to the store, and got them framed. Then I stood them on a bookshelf at home. We had never been one of those families that kept photographs out. But they made me feel a part of a larger something. As I moved around my apartment, I started to become used to seeing my mother, in the cap and gown of her high school graduation, looking out at me. I stared into the eyes of the thin-lipped, strange young man watching me from another picture and searched for signs of the father I knew now.

Eventually, I tracked down some of his old letters. I leafed through my mother's journal for her thoughts about him. I pulled out the old newspaper clippings and read them closely, looking for clues. I called up some of my Dad's old friends and asked them what he used to be like. The bits and pieces I was accumulating slowly began to seem like pieces of a larger mosaic.

I finally came to believe that if I better understood what had happened to my family and my father, it might explain to me how he, and I, had come to be where we were. I wanted to understand who my father was and what he had been long before he ever became my father. I wanted to mark the trail of his life and place it next to my own. I knew where his life would end, but I knew very little about where it had begun. I wanted to know why a boy from a small town in New York State had become an old man in a monk's robe with four children.

It happened almost by accident, but I finally came to see the interviews, the photographs, the letters, the journals, as if they were signposts in a strange land I wanted to explore. Looking at them, following that route, I wanted to see if, by understanding my father, I could better understand myself.

PART TWO
THE FATHER

THREE

✷ ✷ ✷

In his room, my father waited anxiously, listening for the sound of the back door. His father would be home soon. After all these years, Jimmy was going to confront him. He had it all planned out.

It was the spring of 1945, a few days before the eighteen-year-old, a lean young man with big ears, a thin upper lip, and a shy smile, was scheduled to leave for the Army. While he was excited by the adventure that would take him from home for the first time, he worried that his departure would unsettle the precarious emotional balance in his household.

Ever since he could remember, Jimmy had been the fulcrum of his family, an unappointed mediator in an ongoing cold war between his parents and the unofficial protector of his two younger brothers. As a child, he had often lain in bed listening as his parents argued. He thought nothing could be worse, but that was before they stopped speaking to each other at all. For years now, they had lived apart under one roof. They occupied separate bedrooms. They communicated solely through the slam of a door or the slap of a plate on the table. If a noise did not suffice, they addressed each other through the boys. Their life was an elaborate choreography of unstated compromises. His father, for instance, always deposited his weekly paycheck atop the refrigerator; his mother would cash it at the bank and leave her husband his allowance in the same place.

Jimmy's mother, Beatrice, was an insecure, nervous woman. But his father, Michael, was strange to the point of being truly frightening. Mike was prone to sudden, intense rages that frequently threatened to erupt into violence. When he was in the apartment, Bea and the boys were to keep out of his way and stay quiet. Mike rarely spoke to his sons save to snap at them. He never hugged them, offered them advice, or took them anyplace. What little interaction occurred was laced with hostility; after the boys had cleaned the kitchen floor, for instance, their father might track footprints across it out of spite.

Mike spent most days holed up in his room, rocking in his chair, the door closed. He emerged in midafternoon to read the paper while everyone cleared out of the living room. Sometimes he sat on the couch for three hours, while a tense silence filled the apartment.

Most nights at dusk, he left for his job at the U.S. Army depot south of town, where he tended the golf course during the summer and worked as a janitor in the boiler room during the winter. But if it was his night off, the family would enact an unsettling scene that had been played out since Jimmy's early childhood. Bea, Jimmy, Leonard, and Ken would take their places at the table and wait to see if Mike would leave his room and join them. If he deigned to appear, he would sit without a word, then spend the meal glaring straight at Leonard, the middle boy, who closely resembled him. Mike ate little, if at all. Sometimes his dinner would consist of only a cup of tea, in which he would angrily, steadily stir a spoon, over and over. While the spoon clattered, Jimmy and his mother would make idle conversation, pretending nothing was happening. To this day, my father grows unsettled by the sound of a spoon clanging off the sides of a teacup.

Scary as such moments were, Mike had never struck his wife or children. Jimmy thought his father restrained himself because, in some unfathomable way, he respected—or feared—his oldest son. But now that the son was leaving, he suspected his father might not hold back anymore. He had resolved to confront him.

At last, in the early hours of the morning, he heard the screen door slam shut. As always, his mother would have left a plate of food on the stove for her husband. Sometimes Mike just let it sit there. But this night, Jimmy found his father at the table, eating in the dark. He sat down across from him.

Did Mike know Jimmy was going into the Army the next week? Of course he did.

Well, Jimmy had something to tell him before he left. He took a breath, then started speaking. He didn't want anything to happen to his mother or brothers while he was away, he said. He disapproved of his father's behavior.

Mike spit out an explanation. "It's all your mother's fault," he said bitterly. "One day you'll understand." No matter what Jimmy said, his father kept repeating, "It's all your mother's fault."

Finally, Jimmy shot back, using words he'd rehearsed, and which he knew would sting: "I'd rather have a drunkard or a bum for a father" he said "than one like you." With that he stood up, walked away from the table, and went to his room. Mike said nothing.

A few days later Jimmy rose early to catch his train. He kissed his mother. He hugged his brothers. He hoisted his bag around his shoulder. Then he knocked, softly, on his father's bedroom door.

Normally Mike would still be asleep at this early hour, having worked late the night before. But today he was already up and dressed.

He opened the door, then stood in the doorway and didn't say anything. He seemed unsure of what to do. Finally his son stuttered an awkward good-bye and stuck out his hand. Mike looked at it for an instant. Then he threw his arms around him and burst into tears.

※ ※ ※

My father rarely spoke about his childhood when I was growing up. I knew he had been poor and that his family was not close. I knew that, though he was remarkably tolerant of our temper tantrums, he would suddenly and angrily yell when one of us slammed a door, as if a trigger had been pulled, and that his sensitivity was said to stem from his family. More innocently, I knew how he luxuriated in cold and snow, a passion he attributed to a boyhood in Upstate New York. On all but the frostiest nights of winter, he would open the downstairs windows of our house before he went to bed, chilling the rooms so much that sometimes I could see my breath when I came down for breakfast.

Beyond those scraps, however, the details became murky. Dad answered questions incompletely, in one or two short words. He never volunteered information about anyone in his family but his mother. If his brothers came up in conversation, he spoke of them with a combination of remoteness and fondness that made it sound as if they had died long ago in some distant battle. He never referred to his father at all, though I didn't notice the omission. Children view whatever they know as the natural order. It wasn't until I was nine or ten years old that it even occurred to me that I didn't seem to have a grandfather on my father's side of the family.

For that matter, I grew up without much of an extended family at all. My mother was an only child. She had cousins and aunts in New York, but I had only met them a handful of times. My father had never introduced me to his two brothers. Other than occasional visits with my grandmothers, we had no relatives that we felt obligated to see, ever. Our family operated as a self-contained island.

When I recently telephoned my Uncle Leonard out of the blue one day, after tracking him down at his home in Florida, it turned out that his own children had felt the same isolation. "Ours is a strange family," he admitted. "They're not close, they're not emotionally close. They don't discuss things the way

I discuss things with my wife and children. I do not have a picture of my father or any of us as a group, and my kids would not know any of my family if they saw them on the street tomorrow. I find that very strange."

My father grew up in Schenectady, New York, a grubby, working-class city in the eastern reaches of the Mohawk Valley not far from Albany, made up largely of tight rows of squat, wood-framed houses. The two or three visits we made there when I was a boy depressed me. Everything in Schenectady looked dirty and worn-out. The people on the street seemed run-down and tired. My grandmother's infirmities largely confined her to a musty apartment. We could not leave soon enough for me.

My father rarely went back there when I was small. But sometime after he entered the monastery, he began setting aside a few days of his vacations to see his mother. After he had left the city and gotten married, they had grown apart, but now that both were alone and his mother was growing old, he felt an urge to strengthen the bond. For more than a decade, he has been going back home regularly.

One recent summer I went with him. Together we drove past the places where he had lived as a child. Most of them still stood, dilapidated old buildings in poor neighborhoods littered with boarded-up houses and porno shops. The narrow, two-story clapboard house his mother had once owned was still the same shade of yellow that my father and his uncles had painted it in the late 1940s. We wanted to stop, but a group of menacing-looking kids loitered out front, so we merely slowed down to look.

In the 1920s, when my father was born, Schenectady was booming. The city's life in those days revolved around General Electric's enormous turbine-manufacturing complex, which had moved there from New York in 1886 after Thomas Edison sought out a site with room for expansion, lower rents, and less troublesome labor unions. As GE grew through mergers with other electrical companies, the Schenectady plant became the center of the company's power-generation business. In 1930 the census revealed that Schenectady had exploded in several decades from a sleepy backwater to a city of nearly 100,000.

Most of the people my father knew had some connection to the plant. Everyone had a parent or cousin working there. GE's financial condition was a barometer for the health of the entire city. Every year on the Fourth of July my father clambered onto the roof of his Aunt Maude's house for a good view of the GE-sponsored fireworks that climaxed the day's festivities.

By the time he reached college, however, Schenectady had begun a slow decline. GE whittled down employment at the plant over the following decades. Though some of Dad's schoolmates embarked on careers with GE after graduation, more families had started leaving town.

But his mother stayed, and so did his brother Ken, who became an engineer at GE. And so did someone else. After we toured the downtown one morning, my father directed me to a development of concrete apartment buildings a few miles away. When I asked where we were going, he told me it was to see his Aunt Marie.

If I had even known I had an Aunt Marie, I had forgotten. She was his mother's younger sister. I don't think he had been keeping her existence a secret from me. But the reticence he displayed about his childhood naturally segregated his childhood family, including his aunt, from the one I belonged to.

Marie turned out to be a thin, vigorous woman in her mid-eighties. She lived in a tidy one-bedroom apartment with the shades pulled down and the walls and shelves decorated with religious icons. She sat me down at her dining room table, served me a cup of strong coffee, and began to tell me about her family. My father listened on the sofa. At one point, she went to a shelf and pulled down an old Bible. In the frontispiece was a long family tree full of names I had never seen before.

Once she started talking about her girlhood, she even shared one or two stories my father had never heard. Adding these to what he and his brothers had told me, I began to piece together a history of his life, and of my family, that I had never known.

✥   ✥   ✥

My grandmother, Beatrice Audet, was the second of six children born to Oscar and Dora Audet in the first eleven years of the twentieth century. Two of the children died of cholera while they were still small. Oscar's family came from French Canada. He worked as a laborer at the GE plant. Dora came from Troy, New York.

From an early age, Bea was overweight, insecure, and socially awkward. She suffered from several physical infirmities. At the age of three, she lost a finger in a car door. Two years later a bout with polio left her partially lame.

In her better moments, Bea liked to sing and play the piano. Her ear was so good that she could return from a silent movie, sit at the keyboard, and play the tune she had just heard at the theater. She liked makeup and pretty clothes. She organized dancing lessons for her sisters and brothers in the living room.

But she never got along with her parents. The Audets apparently were a somewhat bawdy, even raucous bunch, among whom Bea felt ill at ease. When she was fourteen she either left or was thrown out of the house. She quit school, completing only the eighth grade, and went to work as a telephone operator. For the rest of her life she retained a bitterness toward her family that was apt to flare up at any time. She regularly launched spontaneous, angry diatribes about the injustices she believed she had suffered at their hands.

When Bea was eighteen or nineteen she was briefly engaged to a man whose name no one remembers. After that romance foundered, she began dating a polite, quiet Catholic man whom she considered quite handsome. Michael Murray was ten years her senior. He had what was then considered to be a good job, driving a horse and wagon for Freihofer's bakery.

As the relationship progressed, Bea became eager to wed and start a new life fully out of her parents' shadow. But when the priest finally announced her engagement at mass, he goofed and identified as her betrothed her previous fiancé. Perhaps it was an omen.

Bea and Mike were married on Easter Sunday, 1925, at Sacred Heart Church. I have a photograph of them that was taken that afternoon. Both stand uncomfortably straight, their mouths pursed tightly, their arms to their sides, looking at the camera with grim resolve. It is a bittersweet record of the beginning hours of what would prove to be a profoundly unhappy marriage.

※ ※ ※

Here are the few things I knew about my grandfather's youth: As a boy, he wore long, girlish curls. His father, who had emigrated from Ireland, died when his son was still quite small. Mike grew up devoted to his mother and doted upon by her. Like his future wife, he left school after the eighth grade. He was very religious. As a young man, he attended seminary but only lasted one year.

A photo taken of him just before he joined the Army to fight in the Great War shows him to be a thin, serious-looking but handsome young man. He had wavy brown hair, an endearing if rarely seen smile, and round, wire-rim spectacles.

From the battlefield, he loyally sent all his paychecks home to his mother. But when he returned, he discovered she had married the next-door neighbor during his absence. Feeling betrayed, he refused to move back home with her and instead rented a place of his own. During this period, he developed the habit of taking long walks by himself in the evenings.

People who knew my grandfather well—as well as anyone did, that is—would later say that aloneness was the single characteristic that best described him. My father said his father was one of the loneliest people he ever knew. Mike never had any friends that his sons could recall, didn't even seem to know how to talk to people. He moved through the lives of his family and acquaintances like a shadow.

Something may have happened to him in the war. My uncle showed me an eerie picture of his father from the 1930s. He is still a youthful-looking, lean man, with a sweater draped over his broad shoulders. But he has an oddly blank, empty stare. His mouth is a straight line, his eyes glassy and slightly bulging. It is a terrifying expression, the haunted look of a man who has been shell-shocked. My father remembered seeing that vacant look suddenly come across his father's face once or twice. Even when he was small, he had a sense that something was gone horribly wrong behind those eyes.

Bea did not discover this darker side of her husband until after their whirlwind courtship. But even in their first weeks together, Mike was remote and moody. Bea did not know how to respond to his long bouts of coldness. Emotional where her husband was icy, she sometimes became panicky over her inability to penetrate the fog surrounding him.

Not long after the wedding, Mike was injured in an accident at work in which his horse ran off. He spent weeks at home, shuffling about the house slowly and in great pain, taking a long time to recuperate. One day while Bea was working in the kitchen, he limped past to fetch some pipe tobacco from the bedroom. In the kitchen mirror, she could see his reflection as he moved through the doorway. Out of her sight—he thought—Mike suddenly stood up straight and began moving perfectly normally. Watching him, Bea realized with horror that he had been faking his injuries to avoid returning to work. She began to wonder just how disturbed her husband was. But she was too frightened to say anything to him.

Six months after they married, Bea tried to leave her husband and move back with her parents. But they refused to put her up. They told her she was being a bad wife. To them, Mike Murray was a good catch, a man who didn't drink, didn't cheat, and brought his money home to his wife. Without their support, Bea had few options. Divorce was out of the question, especially for two devout Catholics. The only grounds in New York State was adultery, and neither spouse was the type to have an affair.

With no other prospects, Bea returned. She would end up staying more than twenty years. But the marriage quickly became one to be endured rather than enjoyed. Silently, deliberately, each began to carve out a separate life within the confines of their union, until they lived together almost as ghosts, sharing only a last name and a family.

Bea now turned to her children, especially her firstborn, Jimmy, for meaning. She called the day he was born, October

27, 1926, the happiest of her life. But the intensity of her feelings sometimes manifested itself in deeply disturbing ways. She ascribed to him supernatural abilities and made him a repository for anxieties and even fantasies that reflected her isolation and despair. For years she claimed that he had saved her life by speaking his first words at the age of six months. She would recount how one day the situation seemed so desperate that while Mike was at work she set out to kill herself and the baby. She sealed up the windows and doors and turned on the gas. As the hissing grew louder, she recalled, Jim said to her, "Don't do that, Mom." The son she had been prepared to kill became her savior.

A year after Jimmy was born, Bea had a second son, Leonard. Mike had little to do with either boy. But he was drawn to a third son, Ronald, who was born four years after Leonard. My father, who was five then, dimly recalls his moody father becoming slightly more approachable, at times even cheerful, after Ronnie was born.

But Ronnie came down with spinal meningitis when he was two. One of my father's earliest memories is of a day spent sitting at home, waiting for his mother to return from the hospital. She didn't arrive until he was in bed, bringing a rush of cold air into his room when she opened the door to check on him. Lying there awake, Jimmy asked how Ronnie was. She told him the doctors were feeding him through his nostrils. Jimmy couldn't imagine that. But it sounded bad.

Ronnie died soon afterward. The boys stood by his small casket in the living room as mourners trudged by. With

Ronnie's death, the tiny spark that had been ignited in Mike was extinguished. He became sadder and even more distant.

That same year, 1933, during the depths of the Depression, Mike was fired from his job at the bakery. He didn't work for two years. He refused to hunt for a job. He spent most of his time rocking back and forth in utter silence. He took long walks and ate most of his meals in his room. Whenever Bea tried to talk to him, he listened patiently, then asked, "Are you through?" before stalking out of the house.

The family soon went on relief. Jimmy learned to dread the sound of knocking at the front door. It often signified an angry creditor seeking payment on a bill. More than once he was wakened in the dark to help pack for a sudden move. Dinner frequently consisted of a plate of bread, milk, and sugar. Meat, fruit, or vegetables were a rarity. Jimmy once saw his mother steal some apples from a bushel that had been delivered to a neighbor.

With his father so removed from the family struggles, Jimmy had to help fill the breach. After school, he would strap on his roller skates and wheel several miles to the bakery to buy a loaf of day-old bread for five cents. Often he accompanied his mother to the relief agency to pick up food or clothes. The workers there tended to treat the poor like dirt. Jimmy never forgot the way they seemed to look right through him as if he weren't even present.

The priests and nuns from church weren't any better. None of them came near the run-down flats where the Murrays lived. The only religious people Jimmy ever saw at his house were two Protestant ministers who brought food to the family one Thanksgiving.

If there was a bright spot, it was Bea. Hard times elevated her. Though she remained unsure of herself, she kept the house clean and managed to feed her sons, who now included Kenneth, born in 1932. She told them she loved them and tried to make them feel appreciated despite their father's indifference. They were "Bea and the Boys," and she proclaimed that they would survive their troubles together.

On her own, Bea became an avid reader. She taught herself to cook and made resourceful use of the meager goods handed out by the relief agencies. She looked for ways to bring in extra money. When Jimmy was in junior high school, she baked cookies every Christmas and gave them to him to sell to his teachers. Later, when the boys grew older, she went back to work, first as a nighttime cook at a hospital, then as a telephone operator there.

Jimmy was impressed with her ability to improvise with little. When the boys were small, one flat they lived in was so cold in winter that ice formed on the bedroom walls, thick enough that the boys could write their names in it. Before bedtime, Bea would heat bricks in the oven, then wrap them in towels and slide them under the sheets to keep them warm. Sometime around three o'clock, someone would wake up, realize his brick had gone cold and kick it out of bed. That woke the others, who did the same. The apartment would be filled with the sound of bricks thumping on the floor.

❊ ❊ ❊

To me, it all sounded bleak, almost Dickensian. Yet when I told my father so, he insisted that in many ways his was a happy childhood.

Certainly he was a bright, amiable, and good-natured boy, if something of a loner. From an early age, he possessed a strange inner peace that convinced him he would be protected if he just flung himself out into the world. He followed current events closely, combing his father's newspaper and soaking up Franklin Roosevelt's and Alf Landon's speeches on the radio. He spent hours at the library reading. When he grew older and the family had a little money, he ensconced himself every Saturday morning at the movie house, where he sat entranced through two or three cartoons, a newsreel, a weekly serial, and a double feature. He developed a serious crush on Paulette Goddard.

One of his greatest pleasures was going to church. The pomp and ritual of the mass, the priest with his back to the crowd, waving incense while he muttered sacred and mysterious incantations in Latin, thrilled him and filled him with joy. He reveled in pious practices like the weekly staging of the stations of the cross. He felt an instinctive attraction to the church. Besides the masses on Sunday, he attended lectures on Wednesday nights. Following the lessons he heard, he tried hard to be a good boy.

Adults viewed him as gifted. He did well in school. His parents told him he was the smartest of their boys. When he argued with Leonard, they always took Jimmy's side, even if he was wrong. Much of the favoritism came from Bea, of course, but even Mike more or less directed most of his wrath at his sons.

But the joys and diversions of Jimmy's life were tempered. Anguished over the antipathy between his parents, he worried too about shielding his brothers. He wondered why neither Leonard nor Ken seemed to have the abilities he did. Both struggled in school. Neither possessed Jimmy's optimistic nature.

In social situations, he was solitary and uncomfortable. His academic success and friendliness made him a student leader—he was elected vice president of his senior class in high school—but he only had a couple of friends. He never had a date until his senior prom, when he worked up the nerve to ask out one of the prettiest girls in school, forgetting until they were in the car en route that he didn't know how to dance. He spent most of the night sitting at the table, watching her on the floor with other boys.

He worked hard, and from an early age. His first job was washing dishes at the hospital where his mother worked as a cook. For a while he accompanied his Uncle Dick on his Saturday-morning rounds of fixing slot machines. Next he landed a spot behind the counter at the YMCA. He became friends with some of the men who belonged to the club and through them began to see that there was a world wholly different from his own, a world of tennis matches and classical music and theater that he had barely known existed.

He carried a heavy burden as his mother's friend, helper, confidante, and eventually her virtual coparent. They discussed everything and went everywhere together. She sought his advice on his brothers. When he was nine or ten she began confiding family secrets to him, lifting the curtain on an adult world of extramarital affairs and alcoholism. He considered her the most important person in his life. He frequently reminded his brothers of the sacrifices she made and the difficult life she had led. Both resented his special place in the family yet leaned on him for guidance.

From Bea, he learned two key lessons about his faith. The first concerned the sometimes different standards of behavior demanded by the church. Bea told him she had been denied absolution by her priest for close to two years. She didn't tell him why, but he suspected it had to do with birth control. She knew another woman in a similar bind, she said. Jimmy felt that punishing women for matters they brought up while avoiding these subjects with the men who were also culpable unfairly reduced the former to the status of second-class citizens. The men were not denied absolution. But Bea's second lesson was to separate the flawed humans who ran the church from the institution itself. Whatever questions she had, Bea never lost her faith. This set a powerful example for her son.

Yet as he grew older, Jimmy gradually became disillusioned with the church. He questioned why a fair God made things so hard for his mother and gave Jimmy advantages his brothers lacked. When he asked Catholics why they believed, the response invariably was a rote recitation of dogma, repeated on demand, not an honest explication. He was dismayed by what he perceived as shallowness, sometimes even hypocrisy, in many of the Catholics he met.

Another concern was the increasing strangeness of his father. Since he had gotten the job at the depot, through a neighbor, Mike had at least been bringing in money. But he seemed to be growing even more unbalanced. Though the depot was nearly ten miles away, he insisted on walking to and from work every day, in all kinds of weather. He kept only one chair, his bed, and a prayer book in his bedroom. Once Jimmy caught a quick glimpse of some bizarre religious object he had received in the mail, a heavy belt or something, which he snatched away quickly, then wrapped around his waist under his shirt. Mike didn't even want the family to associate with him in church. Every Sunday he insisted on attending the eleven o'clock high mass alone. He asked his sons and their mother to worship at a different service. And even if the family was short of money that week, he always set aside a dime to present when he entered and a quarter for the collection plate. It was a ritual he had maintained even when he was out of work.

Mike did occasionally ask his oldest son how he was doing. In a strange way, they got along all right. Jimmy felt he understood his father better than anyone else did. Though he feared Mike's temper, he didn't believe Mike was a truly bad man. Occasionally Mike even joined him by the radio to listen to Fred Allen or Jack Benny.

Once, when Jimmy was in high school, his father invited him to a father-son picnic at work. It was the first time Mike had ever extended such an invitation. It turned out to be a total disaster. Mike was shy and faltering. He had nothing to say to any of the other men. It was clear most of them barely knew who he was. Mike and his son had nothing to talk about either. The day was filled with long silences and blank stares, punctuated occasionally by uneasy small talk. To see his father such an outcast at his workplace, Jimmy ached with a mixture of sympathy and humiliation. He had known Mike was moody and troubled. But it wasn't until the picnic that he began to see his father as truly pathetic.

❊   ❊   ❊

Jimmy didn't expect to go to college. His family simply couldn't afford it. But after a counselor at school pushed him to apply for a scholarship, he was amazed to win a one-hundred-dollar award, half of what he needed. Then his father stunned him by giving him the rest. He registered at Union College in Schenectady in the fall of 1944, becoming the first member of his family to advance beyond high school.

But his eighteenth birthday loomed only a few weeks after classes began, and with the war still raging he knew what that meant. His draft notice arrived in the late winter of 1945. He was gone within a few weeks.

Despite his father's tearful good-bye, the breach between them was never repaired. When Jim returned from Europe in the fall of 1946 and moved back home, his financial outlook had been improved by the GI Bill. By then, Bea was making enough money at the hospital to support herself and Ken. Leonard had left home as soon as he turned eighteen. Bea and Jim now decided that she could finally afford to leave her husband. Without telling his father what was going on,

Jim got a loan from school to help his mother make a down payment on a house.

One day, while Mike was at work, Jim helped Bea and Ken pack and move to the new place. Mike came home to an apartment that had been emptied of everything but a table, a chair, a bed, a dresser, and a lightbulb. They left no note.

In the following months, Ken sometimes ran into his father on the street. He was scared of seeing Mike at first, but the encounters were fairly innocent. They fell into slight conversation. Mike always asked Ken how his mother was. Sometimes he slipped his son a twenty-dollar bill to bring home.

Leonard, who had escaped the household at the earliest opportunity, stayed in touch with Mike for years. Though he had absorbed so much of his father's anger, he was the person Mike called for help on the day he came home to find his wife gone. Leonard was the one who went over, helped his father pack his things, and brought him to his sister's house.

With Jim, though, the break was nearly total. Jim avoided his father as much as possible. Mike once sent him a gift while he was in college, and Jim wrote back a thank-you note. Mike proceeded to trumpet the note to friends and relatives as evidence that his son preferred him over his estranged wife. After this story got back to him, Jim never wrote his father again. He saw him once or twice more, by accident. He later ignored Mike's pleas to be invited to his wedding.

Today he considers the confrontation with his father to

be one of the pivotal moments of his life. For him, it marked the beginning of his adulthood in as stark a way as possible. I think the episode also helped free him, his brothers, and his mother to build new lives for themselves. Someone had confronted their fearsome father, and instead of lashing back, he had crumbled.

But it's harder to gauge the lasting effects of my grandfather's sad life on my father. Mike Murray certainly served as an example of how not to be as a husband and parent. He passed on to his son a sense that the world is not a happy place. At the same time, my father's penchant for solitude, perhaps some of his deep religious inclination, might be traced to his own father. So might his ability, from an early age, to keep the world at a distance, to shield himself from becoming too attached to things or people.

Though my father is a reflective man, he claims not to spend much time looking back at his father today. "I think about him from time to time," he once told me. "But he just was not a satisfactory father or husband, that's all. He was a failure and it was sad. I chose right, and I've never regretted it."

After the family left him, Mike lived with his sister for some months. He eventually made his way to Hartford, Connecticut, where he worked as a maintenance man at the Pratt & Whitney Corporation and a security guard in a bank. Mike died of a heart attack in 1977. My father did not even know he had been ill until afterward.

After he left home, Dad tried to preserve his ties to his mother but put his childhood behind him. He felt responsible for her happiness and worried constantly over her welfare. He angrily defended Bea against relatives who blamed her for the collapse of her marriage. He wrote long letters to comfort her, filled with praise and assurances that she was not insignificant.

From Europe in 1946, he wrote:

> *Remember when you used to bake your own bread? I guess we were poor then, but a kid doesn't remember how much money the family had—he just remembers the things he liked. I have a lot of memories of things I liked—your cooking was only one of them. I liked it just before the holidays when we were wrapping presents and you were baking cookies & cake. Remember when you used to sell cookies? I used to like to stand in front of the kitchen stove and watch you work. I liked the wisdom you used in bringing us up—still don't know how you could get married so young and know how to bring us up and teach kids so well. Used to like it when you'd take us to church. Used to like to surprise you by cleaning the house or do part of the ironing when you were out. Liked to have you come back from downtown bringing in the fresh air with you and liked to poke thru the packages you'd bring home. Liked to play football or baseball all day and come home to a hot meal. Liked to lie awake in bed and listen when you had the gang over for cards or bingo. Liked to hear you sing as you went about your housework. Liked to listen to the steady hum of the sewing machine on sewing days.*

Liked to have you stay home nights and read a good book. . . .

. . . I like to remember—it's just as well, too, cause when I get back things will be different—I'm grown up now. I can say, though, that I cherish and will always cherish every moment of my childhood—both good and bad. And, I can say I love you for what you have done for us. Guess I'll have to silently close the book on my childhood—all memories now, and start building castles in the air for my own future kids. . . .

As she grew older, my grandmother's life turned increasingly inward. She cultivated few friends. When she retired from her hospital job in the early 1960s, she skipped her own party, even refusing a taxi her coworkers sent to pick her up.

But she endured, stubborn and implacable, with a firmness and will that could be exasperating but at times also admirable. She relished being alone in her apartment, as if it were a piece of territory that she had fought all her life to carve out and defend. She seemed to luxuriate in the privacy and control she had finally gained for herself. Even when her children or grandchildren came by, she sometimes greeted them at the door by saying, "Oh, it's you," and treating their presence as an imposition. Three of her favorite words became: "Leave me alone." Her faith deepened. She frequently went to mass with her younger sister, Marie. She and Mike never divorced.

For years, she kept a pocket-sized zodiac and birthday book, which I now have. Its scratched, brown-cloth cover is framed by frayed pieces of masking tape; many of its pages are falling out. Throughout the book, my grandmother has noted the pivotal events over seventy years in her life and the lives of her loved ones, some of them in the cribbed handwriting of an old woman with arthritis:

January 17: Mother's Birthday, died, June 13, 1956, gone but never forgotten.

January 29: Jim & Michele Married 1955.

March 12: Ronald Mark Died, 1933, born April 30, 1931. MY BABY.

March 14: Michele died this day, 1974 (Thursday)

May 22: Leonard Audet (gone—May 28, 1956). Rest in peace, Brother.

July 19: Me, myself.

July 26: Started working at hospital, 1941, 36 years old. Lived at 406 Schenectady St.

July 27: Mike's, 1895.

October 3: Teeth out, 1956.

She wrote regularly to my father, especially after he went to live at the abbey. Usually they were short letters, just a few paragraphs long, with her thoughts about us children or complaints about her failing health. She told him, "Nothing in my whole life has given me the joy of your new and Holy life." She sent gloves, handkerchiefs, prayers—and advice. "In my life," she once wrote, "there have been decisions I've made and things that I've done, that I'd give a lifetime to undo." Also encouragement: "You are the kindest, most unselfish person I have ever known," she wrote during the time when our home was breaking up. "Your children do not take after you at all."

By then she had reached her eighties. She had phlebitis and high blood pressure. Her mobility lessened after a hip replacement in 1982. A series of nurse's aides passed through her apartment. She began to dread the prospect of moving to a nursing home and having to live with other people, but after several years of minor crises, it became clear to my father and his brother Ken that there was no alternative.

During long, sometimes anguished conversations on the telephone, Dad and his brother reconnected for the first time in four decades. With their mother becoming incapacitated, Dad began staying with Ken and his wife, Joyce, during his annual summer trips to Schenectady. They started setting aside a few days to see each other every year. Ken, a nonpracticing Catholic who is amazed that my father became a monk, even took the train out to the abbey once or twice.

Though they have little to talk about, they seem comforted simply being in each other's presence. Ken has a rasp similar to my father's but is clean-shaven, with a collar of receding hair around his scalp, a wry smile, and a lean frame. He is six years younger than my father but looks older. He enjoys simple pleasures: watching television, working in his garden, spending time with his grandchildren.

❊ ❊ ❊

At least once during my father's trips home, the two brothers will hop in the car for the hourlong drive to see their mother.

Not long after she entered the rest home, my grandmother began showing signs of Alzheimer's disease. By the time Dad became a priest, an event she had eagerly awaited for years, she no longer knew who he was.

During my visit, I joined them on their annual pilgrimage. It was a hot afternoon in July, a few days before my grandmother's birthday. I sat in the backseat, holding a box of hard candies we'd bought for her. It would be my first visit with my grandmother since I was seventeen, when I stopped to see her on my way to a college admissions interview with my brother. She had been in the hospital that time, too.

The rest home was in Troy, New York. Inside, the hushed hallways were cluttered with old people scattered about in their wheelchairs. Their eyes followed me, my father, and my uncle as we passed.

Ken and Dad kept commenting on how clean the place was and how fortunate their mother was to have ended up here. "I've never gone over here when Mother hasn't looked like a queen," Ken said as we rode up in the elevator. I kept quiet, but I was thinking they were crazy. This place was grim and sad. I felt sorry Grandma was ending her life here.

My grandmother lived in Room 310. When we arrived, we found another woman in a wheelchair blocking the doorway, staring straight ahead and still as a statue. She looked as if she had started to wheel herself out for a ride but after a short distance figured, "Why bother?" We paused uncomfortably but said nothing. With what seemed like great effort, she lifted her chin and smiled. "Do you want to get in here?" she asked.

We thanked her as she wheeled forward and allowed us past. I could see a form lying in the far bed, by the wall. The face was blocked from our view by the divider.

Two years before, when my father came to see her, my grandmother had been able to sit in a chair to welcome him. She hadn't known who he was but had recognized that he was a relative and had asked as he entered, "Are you my son, my husband, or my brother?" She could say a prayer for him then. Even a year earlier, she could still sit up in bed for his visit.

This year she lay lost in the folds of her blanket, a shriveled figure in a flowered nightgown. Everything she owned was in this corner of the room. Across from the foot of her bed stood a dresser. On top sat a television set and a vase of flowers. A bulletin board hung on the wall above it, with a birthday card from Leonard thumbtacked to it, next to a picture of my cousin Ken's wedding from the year before. On the side wall hung a red plastic cross, donated by the Salvation Army, and a small picture of a beneficent, glowing Jesus. Photos covered a second bulletin board next to her bed, most of them connected in some way to my father: a few recent portraits of him in his black monk's robe, some snapshots of his ordination ceremony, a couple of postcards of Saint Bede.

As we greeted my grandmother, her roommate wheeled back into the room and turned on her own television. She stared at the screen as a young, good-looking couple French-kissed on *As the World Turns*.

Grandma's white hair was combed out on the pillow

around her like a crown. The mottled skin on her face was pulled tight like leather. Branches of blue veins rippled across her forehead. Her upper teeth were missing, and when she spread her mouth and crinkled her eyes to smile, her lower four teeth jutted up like stalagmites. It wasn't always clear by her expression if she was laughing or crying.

Her left hand, the one with the index finger missing, quivered above the bedding. She frequently drew it to her mouth. Her right arm, one of the limbs stricken by her polio nearly eighty years before, lay at her side or crept up reflexively to rub her belly; it seemed to move of its own will. Under the blanket, her legs came together like a V and then seemed to disappear. By the shape, it looked like she had a mermaid's tail instead of legs.

My father stood at one side of the bed, my uncle at the other. I kept a distance, unsure of what to say. Each of them leaned over and kissed her on the forehead. They smiled down at her. "Do you know who we are?" asked Ken. We didn't wait for an answer but told her our names. "You staying out of trouble?" he asked.

"Oh, yes," she said, then laughed. "They don't always like to talk to me because I'm crabby," she said with some pride, and laughed again.

Ken leaned over and smiled. "Your birthday's coming up," he said. "Do you know how old you're going to be?"

"Oh, no," she said, sounding genuinely worried.

"You're going to be ninety-two."

"Oh, my."

She chattered for the twenty or so minutes of our visit,

and I couldn't understand much of what she said. We smiled and shook our heads and said, "Yes," a lot. She kept grinning and grabbing my father's hand and holding it to her mouth. He rubbed her hands fondly with his left hand and brushed her hair back with his right. Her voice was a thin, reedy croak. She seemed to be in good spirits, though she complained several times about being lame. She kept asking each of us, "What's your name?"

At one point, Dad took a recent photograph of himself from his wallet and handed it to her. She clutched it firmly and smiled. Uncle Ken smiled too as he asked her, "Do you know who that is?"

"Is it my mother?" she asked.

"No, it's your son. That's Jimmy." He pointed at my father. "That's him."

"Oh." She carefully held up the picture and compared it with the man standing next to her. "You're a very handsome man."

Ken showed her another photograph, one he'd taken from her bulletin board. It showed Dad holding my nephew Nicholas when he was only a few months old. "That's your great-grandson," I told her, glad to have something to say.

She clutched the photo in her left hand and shook it firmly. "Beautiful, beautiful," she said to my uncle.

He pointed at my father and said, "That's his grandson."

Still, she kept talking to Ken, saying, "Beautiful, beautiful."

Dad asked, "Mother, would you like me to say a prayer for you?"

"Oh, yes."

Dad got down on his knees and took a firm grip of her left hand with his own. He tenderly caressed her forehead with his knuckles. Ken drifted down to the foot of the bed and stood uncomfortably, half looking at the wall. I stood between them, feeling awkward and trying to just blend in. I always feel uneasy when my father starts to pray.

Dad thanked God for the new light of this day, for the chance to have another day of life. Grandma smiled as he prayed but started talking during his pauses and periodically interrupted him with unintelligible words. Calmly, he'd wait for her to finish before proceeding with prayers. He said an Our Father for her, and a Hail Mary, which he altered slightly to ask, "Holy Mary, Mother of God, pray for Beatrice and those who love her."

When he finished, Grandma began talking again. She seemed to be reliving some old family sorrows. I thought I heard something about her lameness again, and how her mother threw her out of the house when she was fourteen. "It was a hard life," she said finally.

"Yes, but you got through it," my father said, smiling at her. "You outlived them all."

She smiled up at him gratefully. "What's your name again?"

"Jimmy. I am your son. I am a father. I have four children. I have two grandchildren. But I am also a monk and a priest."

"Oh," she said. She paused, looking reflective. "You had a good mother," she finally said.

"I did have a good mother. I had an outstanding mother. And do you know who that mother was?"

"No."

He stroked her forehead again. "You. You were an outstanding mother."

"Me?" She smiled. Her shiny eyes crinkled.

After a minute of silence, she thoughtfully said, "Wouldn't it be nice if we were all sisters?"

By then, it was clear she was getting a little worn-out. We thought we should leave and let her rest. "Thank you for coming to see me!" she cried out as we said good-bye. She pulled my father in for a kiss on the lips and one on the forehead, and he held on to her hand tightly for a moment.

As we turned to leave, she asked him, "What's your name again?"

"Jimmy. I'm your son—and that's your son." Ken waved good-bye to her from the foot of the bed.

We rode down the elevator in silence. Downstairs, Ken wanted to stop in the cafeteria. We got drinks and sat at a round table in the back. No one spoke.

Finally, my uncle said, "She was tough." He shook his head sadly. "She couldn't move her arm or her left leg, you know. She was lame. But she did everything. She used to drive. She taught herself to drive late in life. She'd pick up her leg and move it over to put it down on the pedal."

He bent over and grabbed his left leg to demonstrate.

FOUR

※ ※ ※

In the winter of 1954, my father arrived for the first meeting of his Herman Melville class fifteen minutes early and full of excitement. He hadn't come to spear the great white whale. He was looking for a girl.

The previous fall, the twenty-seven-year-old Jim had taken a writing class at the New School for Social Research in New York. There had been a young woman in the class who attracted him, a buxom, bubbly brunette. She was not conventionally beautiful. She had slightly thick lips and an awkward shape. She wore glasses. But she exuded intelligence, charm, talent, and vigorous engagement with the world. Every week she tumbled into the classroom, books and magazines spilling from her arms, ideas and opinions and experiences pouring from her lips as she whisked off her shawl and sat down. Her stories, when read by the teacher, were thoughtful, ambitious, and sensitive, despite their roughness. She wasn't shy about sharing her strong opinions. She wouldn't hesitate to argue with the teacher or criticize somebody else's work.

Jim had quietly watched her from his seat. He found her

far more appealing than most other girls. While they might have prettier faces, few had anything interesting to say. This girl, Michele, did. The problem was that while he had gotten to know her slightly, he had never found the right time to ask her out. He couldn't tell if he had even made any impression on her at all.

Though Jim had been on his own for years now, he had never been much of a dater and had little confidence in his appeal. He had almost no money to spend on girls. His parents' relationship had made him wary of romance. But he was lonely. He longed for someone to whom he could open up.

Late in the semester, he had overheard Michele telling friends that she planned to take a Melville class that winter. The teacher was the noted critic Alfred Kazin. Jim had signed up, too.

And so, not long after Christmas, he found himself sitting in an empty classroom on a cold evening, waiting for Michele to arrive. Amazingly, she was the second person to show up. They were alone. She recognized him. They had to talk to each other. Each said hello. They made polite conversation. And this time Jim finally worked his way around to asking her on a date.

She said yes. She agreed to go out with him that Friday.

Jim was elated. As Kazin and the rest of the students shuffled in, as everyone settled into their seats and took out their notebooks and class began, he sat at his desk wondering where he should take Michele.

And after that first hour ended, he never bothered returning to Kazin's Melville class.

She was a spirited, flighty, opinionated, insecure, cocky, precocious, wise, immature, and paradoxical burst of energy out of Borough Park in Brooklyn. She was a Jew who had converted to Catholicism, a highbrow intellectual aspirant from a working-class family, an independent-minded woman with a girlish longing for love and a naiveté about sex. Jim had never met anyone like her.

Judith Michele Freedman had been born in April 1933 into an Orthodox Jewish household headed by Archie Freedman, known as Augie, and his wife, Mollie. She was raised as an only child. Her younger brother, Alan, had died of spinal meningitis in his infancy. Her father died of a liver ailment when she was eight. The family had been strictly kosher and dutifully religious, but after Augie died they instantly stopped going to synagogue and shed all religious practices. Judy and her mother moved into an apartment together. To support them, Mollie, a tough, slightly acerbic, and bright redhead, had to take a drab post as a legal secretary for her younger brother, Sid.

Mollie's mother, Fannie, also moved in with them. A widow who had once run a candy store with her husband, Julius, on the Lower East Side of Manhattan, Fannie was the only member of her family who still lit candles on Friday nights. Judy and her grandmother were very close, especially with Mollie often working six days a week and sometimes late into the evening. With her mother, Judy seems to have had one of those intense mother-daughter relationships in which currents of abiding love alternate with episodes of bitter anger. Both were stubborn, emotional women prone to occasional hysterical fits. One day when she was about nine, Judy came home to discover that her mother had thrown all her toys away. Throughout her adolescence, they bickered constantly.

Judy's unusual intelligence and fierce independence stamped her as the family rebel. Among her cousins, aunts, and uncles, she became known for her passions and wild notions. She felt smarter than everyone else around her, and in many ways she was. She decided at an early age that she would become a great artist and began to read and write with fervor. She had read deeply in the classics by the time she finished high school. She borrowed classical-music records from the library, playing them loudly enough to irritate her mother. She wrote precocious poems with titles like "Caprice in Onyx and Amber" and "Moment from a Masque" ("The silent swans greet twilight/As the weeping willow sings"). When her mother told her she should be spending more time learning to cook, Judy shot back, "The man I'm going to marry is also reading books right now."

From an early age she nurtured a rich fantasy life. She envisioned a crowded future in which she would be, simultaneously, a brilliant writer, passionate wife, and devoted mother. As she grew older, she became driven to achieve her ambitious dreams and increasingly distanced from her family.

Judy embraced New York's cultural life with zest. She regularly traveled into the city to attend the ballet, see foreign films, and eat Japanese food. She joined the horde of screaming girls who mobbed the sidewalk in front of the Paramount Theater to swoon over Frank Sinatra. She packed herself into the bleachers at Ebbets Field to see her beloved Brooklyn Dodgers, whose lineup and player stats she memorized.

She was not shy. At fifteen, she wrote an essay extolling Laurence Olivier's film adaptations of *Hamlet* and *Henry V,* judging them to be "true art." She forwarded a copy of the essay to the actor, who in early 1949 wrote a brief response to Miss Freedman, thanking her for her "charming letter" and "your essay on 'Hamlet' on my essay on 'Hamlet.' I was most interested to read it, and much delighted that I seemed to come out of it all right." Not satisfied to end the correspondence there, she wrote a follow-up. I don't have a copy of it, but it seems to have contained some unsolicited career advice. In a slightly aggravated but bemused, tone, Olivier wrote back. "I am afraid that at the moment an opportunity does not present itself for a repertory season in New York. But it is extremely kind of you to offer your suggestions."

She mirrored her precocity with a youthful romanticism. In the voluminous journal she began on her sixteenth birthday, she depicted herself early on as a "writer" and an "artist." In September of 1950, when she was all of seventeen, she selected as her lifelong literary themes "the timelessness of time, the power of love, and the motivation for the tragic actions of humanity." She railed against modern critics who "have renounced humanity and profess to be its experts." She regularly made resolutions. In November of that year, she dramatically declared: "I will not marry, ever, I know. I shall live alone, growing older and dryer and poorer.

I shall kill myself in the rose bushes or go mad from my eternal daydreams of great love in the years. I try to have a future, but it is all a dream. . . ."

Such remarks reflected the sensitive, self-doubting side of her personality. For all her intellectual confidence, she hated her looks and wondered whether any boys would ever find her attractive. She was passionately jealous of a beautiful cousin and felt she had been cheated by fate. Her innate dislike of her body eventually would grow to outright loathing.

Shortly before Michele finished high school, Mollie remarried, to an Estonian socialist and shopkeeper named Sam Solomon. A plainspoken man with simple tastes and vivid memories of pogroms and the 1905 revolution, Sam regularly clashed with his strong-willed, melodramatic stepdaughter. He thought she was spoiled. She thought he was simple-minded. They battled for months before Sam moved the family to his home in Washington, D.C., where he ran a grocery store. Judy accompanied them but only so she could start classes at American University. It was the one college to which they could afford to send her. As soon as classes started, she went to live on campus.

At the time, American University was little more than a commuter college. Most of the students were night students. Judy later resented the fact that her family couldn't provide a better education for her. Socially, the atmosphere was still fairly square in those days. Judy found it to be a somewhat innocent world of sorority parties, student societies, and backseat gropes.

On campus she shed the loathsome name Judy and introduced herself as Michele. One group of friends nicknamed her Maggie. As always, Michele impressed her fellow students with the force of her intellect and her thirst for books. She joined the New Democrats, where she enthusiastically touted Adlai Stevenson for president. She set out on a heartfelt but frustrating search for true love. Her journals and letters record her repeated efforts to unearth a soul with whom she could commune, only to end up stuck with a slobbering sophomore who just wanted to sleep with her. She punctuated periods of romantic swooning with disgusted declarations in which she swore off men to devote herself to art.

Among her close friends was a woman named Joanne Greenberg, who would later write the novel *I Never Promised You a Rose Garden*. I called Joanne, who lives in Colorado today, and she told me my mother struck her as "a very straightforward Brooklyn Jewish intellectual at the wrong school. There were maybe five of us on campus who were considered the intellectuals at the time. She was very much the strongest of us all."

In 1951, when she was eighteen, Michele began to question her religious faith after years of nonbelief. She recorded growing intimations of a higher power. In typically methodical fashion, she read dozens of books, sought out clergy, enthusiastically tried to pray as books instructed. One Catholic priest who aided was a Jewish convert who became active in Catholic-Jewish relations. She absorbed the works of such writers as François Mauriac, Jacques Maritain, Thomas Merton, Martin Buber, G. K. Chesterton, Simone

Weil, C. S. Lewis, and Graham Greene; the Catholics among them were writers who were sweeping campuses in a brief revival of Catholicism that sprouted after the war.

She finally reached a dramatic conclusion. "Suddenly, but not so suddenly, I have thought and evaluated to the point that I believe in Christ's sacrifice on the cross for the redemption of humanity," she wrote that November. "But I cannot believe in his Divinity . . . where can I go from here?"

By February 1953, two months before her twentieth birthday, she had her answer; she would become a Roman Catholic. The news stunned her friends and family. "I nearly fell over dead," Joanne Greenberg told me, "because she seemed so Jewish to me. This happens commonly now, but it didn't happen then. It was a big deal." Mollie wouldn't stop crying when Michele broke the news. She said it was her fault for failing to keep a kosher household and provide her daughter a proper Jewish upbringing. She feared she had lost Michele for good.

Staggered by the depth of her mother's dismay, Michele spent weeks praying, talking to priests, deepening her reading in Catholic thought, and writing anguished letters explaining her decision to relatives and friends. Ironically, her biggest defender in the family turned out to be her grandmother, Fannie, the only practicing Jew. "If you don't support her," Fannie warned her children and grandchildren, "you will lose her."

Under Fannie's influence, the family finally seems to have accepted the conversion by classifying it as another of Michele's crazy ideas. She was baptized on campus on May 8,

1953, a ceremony she called "the most exciting news of all for me not only for today but for my life, I guess."

The conversion came on the cusp of a new life for her. That autumn she returned to New York. She found an apartment on the Upper East Side and signed up for classes at the New School for Social Research. It was only a few months later, on February 13, 1954, that she recorded some exciting news in her journal.

"Maybe my luck has broken, at least temporarily, because I went out on a date last night and had a really terrific time!" she wrote. "The boy was James Murray, who was in my writing class last semester and is in my Melville class this semester and who also has writing ambitions."

※ ※ ※

Meeting Michele was easily the best thing to happen to Jim in the decade after he left home to join the Army. For him, those were years mostly filled with frustrations and false starts.

The train that carried my father from Albany to Fort Dix in early 1945, literally transporting him away him from the deprivations and sorrows of his childhood, was the first he had ever ridden. Like other young recruits, he was abstractly worried about being killed or injured in battle but mostly thrilled to join a great adventure that lifted the curtain on a wider world. During basic training, he met boys from all parts of the country, heard for the first time stories about life in the South and the West. He relished the release from the tensions and responsibilities of home. He didn't even mind Army food.

His military career was undistinguished. He was a poor soldier. Assigned to the heavy-weapons unit, he felt ill at ease with a gun in his hand and couldn't shoot straight. A high score on an exam won him a chance to study Japanese at the University of Minnesota, but soon after he arrived, the war ended and the program collapsed. He reenlisted as a technician, ranked one level below a sergeant, and went to Marburg, Germany. For a little more than a year, he worked as a personnel clerk, delivering orientation talks to new recruits and processing paperwork for departing veterans. The job was mostly a grind: In one letter home, he reported that his group had processed 1,078 men in one day and faced the prospect of another 800 the next.

But the Army did open new doors. In Germany, he met men who liked classical music and men who read great literature. Under their influence, he taught himself about Bach and Mozart. A friend lent him a copy of *The Magic Mountain,* and it mesmerized him. He picked up the works of other German novelists, then poets. He started reading newspapers and magazines to follow domestic politics and the rapidly emerging shape of the postwar world. He thought he had discovered within himself a vague, previously unnoticed yearning to write. Skills he possessed, particularly his childhood ability to conjure up people and bits of conversation in his head, led him to think he might have a gift for it.

He had fallen away from the church, but he remained straitlaced almost to the point of self-righteousness. When a couple of friends who were having problems with their girl-friends came to him for advice, he counseled them to become Christians. He once accompanied his closest buddy to dinner at the home of his buddy's German girlfriend, but when he found out his friend and the girl were sleeping together, he refused to return. He found he liked many of the Germans he met and felt moved by the devastation of their country. On leave, he traveled to Rome and toured the Vatican, where he caught a brief glimpse of Pope Pius XII.

When he got back home, Jim reenrolled at Union College and switched his major from premed to English literature. He felt himself swept up in a tide of returning GI's who were getting a shot at a college degree for the first time, transform-ing a diploma from an upper-crust credential to a middle-class rite of passage. College was the first place he had felt completely happy. He started reading Henry James and worked his way through the great Russian and German novel-ists, developing an abiding passion for Dostoyevsky. Though he rarely dated, he built a small circle of friends for the first time in his life, who shared his growing interest in books and music. He earned good grades and became editor of the school newspaper. He began to nurture what seemed a ridiculous plan for a poor kid from a working family: mov-ing to New York to write a novel.

Throughout his college years, Jim lived at home with his mother in the house he helped her buy. Reminders of his poverty-stricken childhood were unavoidable. Once, an old Army buddy called to say he was passing through Schenec-tady with his parents and wanted to come by for a visit. Bea spent the day cleaning the house and preparing a big meal. But when Jim's friend pulled up, his parents took one look at the house and refused to come inside. Jim's friend tried to talk him into going out and looking for girls instead. Hurt and deeply embarrassed for his mother, Jim refused.

Yet as the end of college approached, he tried subtly to lessen his mother's dependence on him. Though he determined to be there for her, he worried that if he wasn't careful, her overwhelming needs would keep him from breaking away. He began to share fewer details of his life. He affected a slight coolness, deploying the emotional distance he had developed as a child. He told himself the world of artists he aspired to join had little in common with the impoverished one he was leaving behind. Bea was hurt, and privately skeptical about his writing ambitions. But she told her son she understood why he wanted to leave.

Not long after he graduated in the summer of 1950, Jim hewed to his plan and moved to Manhattan. He gave himself two years in which to have a novel written and published.

He stayed for several weeks in a boardinghouse on West Eighty-fifth Street, then found a cheap apartment on West Forty-eighth. He worked his way through a series of low-paying jobs in a matter of months. First he washed dishes in a restaurant far out on Long Island. Then he spent a few months behind the counter at a coffee shop in Grand Central Station, working the overnight shift. His coworkers were suspicious of him because he was the only employee who didn't steal from the cash drawer (one had taken enough money to buy a small airplane). The following

February, one of his regulars at the coffee shop, a linotype operator, got him a job as a copyboy at the New York *Daily News*. It seemed like it could be the first leg of a writing career. But copyboys made just twenty-six dollars a week, not enough to live on. Jim learned that the other copyboys supplemented their salaries by cheating on their expense vouchers, charging the paper for taxi rides, for instance, when they had taken the subway. He wouldn't do it despite his boss' pleas, and had to quit within two months. He finally landed a job as a bank teller at Manufacturers Trust Company, on Third Avenue and Eighty-fifth Street.

By this time, Jim's adventure was starting to wear thin. He had been in New York for more than six months and had little money and few friends to show for it. Even worse, he had no novel. He discovered he lacked the discipline to regularly sit at his typewriter. What he produced there was flat. Despite his imagination and his interest in big themes, he couldn't conjure up plausible characters or craft a cohesive narrative. He became lonely and moody. Forty years later he diagnosed himself to me as a lonely neurotic who lacked confidence in his abilities.

He never attended church and did not think much about religion. But he did have a sudden, strange encounter that he later viewed as pivotal. One night, as he lay in bed trying to fall asleep, he had the odd sensation that a black presence was trying to come through the window to reach him. It made no sense, but he had no time to analyze it: He suddenly felt nervous, then panicky, short of breath. He began to struggle. He was choking. Amid gasps, he instinctively began reciting the Our Father. The presence instantly vanished. He relaxed.

What did the presence mean? Though he never saw it again, he dreamed about it periodically over the next few years. And though he had left the church, he believed it was a demon. He didn't know what it wanted with him, but the entire experience demonstrated to him that deep down he retained belief in God.

In the spring of 1952 Jim received a letter from Bea in which she noted that Ken, who had had some nervous problems ever since he'd had rheumatic fever as a child, was in poor health. Jim volunteered to move back home for a while to help. Though he feigned some reluctance, he was secretly relieved. He knew he had failed as a writer. Two years into his two-year plan, he had nothing to show for his efforts.

Back in Schenectady, Jim got work as a teller at the Schenectady Savings Bank and spent his evenings holed up in his room, reading short stories and novels that he ordered through the mail from the New School. Slowly he regained some confidence, while his artistic cravings became reignited. When Ken seemed better after nearly a year, Jim concluded that he would rather fail as a writer than succeed as anything else.

Without any prospects, he returned to Manhattan in the fall of 1953. He rented an apartment on the edge of Greenwich Village, on Fifteenth Street between Sixth and Seventh Avenues. Carrying a letter of recommendation from his old boss, he found another teller's job at Broadway Savings Bank at Twenty-third Street and Eighth Avenue. It paid thirty-five dollars a week with a hot lunch every day. Determined to make one last stab at writing, Jim signed up for classes at the New School. It was only a few weeks until he met the woman who was to become his wife.

※　※　※

On their first date, Michele dragged Jim to a meeting of a Catholic literary society she had joined, hoping to impress him. But when she asked Jim what he thought, he told her he thought the group was exploiting her because she was a convert. She didn't go back. Afterward, he took her to an apartment on the Lower East Side, where she met some of his friends and drank bourbon and water. Michele liked the people but was most taken by their Siamese cat. From there, they rode to another friend's place, on Fortieth Street between Second and Third avenues and didn't make it home until four in the morning. Outside Michele's apartment, they shared "a really cozy kiss," she wrote in her journal. It had been a "nice time, for no particular explainable reason, just because every ingredient of an otherwise normal evening clicked in the right way."

Jim found her intelligent and talkative, interested in politics, literature, history, religion. It was stimulating, if intimidating to him. He sometimes felt ill-educated and shy next to her. But he also was stable and even-tempered where she was mercurial. He grounded her. She was impressed that he listened to what she said, respected her opinion, and seemed to want more than sex from her. He was glad to have someone who understood his writing ambitions, his unhappiness over his family, and his loneliness.

They initially dated every other weekend but soon kept standing engagements every Wednesday and Saturday. It quickly became serious. Michele soon started speaking as if the two were naturally going to be married and on one early date even dragged Jim out to Long Island to meet her cousins and forced him to pose with her for some family photographs. They saw Japanese kabuki dancers and went to the circus, rode the Ferris wheel at Coney Island, and watched *The World of Sholem Aleichem* on Broadway. They double-dated with his friends and held hands at the movies. Each date ended with long sessions of necking.

"I needn't act with him at all," Michele wrote in her journal in April. "We can pleasantly disagree and argue, we can talk seriously, or, as late last night, just get slap happy in perfect comfort . . . it is a pleasant change to have all this with a person who has intelligence and similar interests and, on a more superficial level, is polite and pleasant."

Through Michele's eyes, Jim caught his broadest glimpse yet of the world of books and art. He was intrigued by her newfound faith. She had come to it through literature and theology that were at the other end of his own experience with the church. She seemed to have come to Catholicism from on high; for Jim, it remained at best a habit of childhood. While he still wouldn't return to the church, he found her enthusiasm for religion infectious.

On April 21, four days before Michele's twenty-first birthday, the two spent the evening sitting by the river, drinking beer, and talking. Afterward, Michele went home and confessed in her journal, "He is a dear, sweet boy . . . and I do love him very much—there—I've said it!"

In early May Michele won a two-year fellowship to complete her master's degree in English literature at the University of Connecticut at Storrs. She took the news to Jim, partly hoping he would try to persuade her to stay with him. Instead, he told her it was an opportunity she couldn't pass up and encouraged her to go. She was devastated. An argument broke out—and ended with Jim declaring his love. By August, as she prepared to move, Michele was writing a friend: "Jim is eager to get married, as eager as a dog on a short leash, and I think my going away is going to make him more and more eager." Jim didn't know it, but she had already picked out china and silver patterns.

One day in early October, just a month after Michele had left, Jim asked his boss for an afternoon off from work, hopped a bus up to Storrs, found his way to Michele's room, surprised her at her door, and proposed that they get married that winter. He would quit his job and move there, he said. "I am so happy I am numb!" Michele wrote that night.

For the next five months, they communicated through the mail. Most days ended with each sitting down after work to write the other. After they parted at the end of weekend visits, each would immediately write out some thoughts about what had just transpired and drop them in the mailbox. They probably belonged to the last generation of young Americans who wrote so many love letters.

His letters often ran for pages. Sometimes he typed them and sometimes he scrawled them in barely legible handwriting on sheet after sheet of school notebook paper. Usually he mailed them immediately so they would reach her the next day. He wrote her about New York State politics, which he watched closely during that election season. He wrote about problems afflicting his friends, complaining about one who, though married, persuaded Jim to lend him his apartment for liaisons with his mistress. He wrote about movies he saw and parties he attended. He wrote about the meals he had just eaten before sitting down at his desk and sometimes noted how many "cigs" he had smoked that day. He wrote about the '47 black Pontiac he bought from someone at the bank. He wrote suggestions for the guest list at the wedding. He wrote about the books he was reading, including Stendhal's *The Red and the Black*, F. Scott Fitzgerald's *The Crack-Up,* and most of the works of Joseph Conrad, which he raced through that autumn. For a while, everything made him think of Conrad.

He wrote in great detail about his halting efforts at fiction. He even sent her two stories, "The Cat" and "The Key," and countless notes about and pages from his novel. Laying out his scheme for the book, he noted, "Everything is there except my ability."

As the wedding date approached, he wrote increasingly about religion. Michele wanted a church wedding. Jim still did not want to return, but he had begun trying to grope his way toward some religious insight. Throughout his writing, and under Michele's influence, he was exploring religious themes and challenging his beliefs for the first time in a decade.

Michele listened as he explained his reasons for staying away, but the pastor in Storrs was less tolerant. He ordered Jim to meet with a Jesuit priest in New York, Father Finlay, to talk about his faith and receive instruction. Jim found the two-hour meetings intellectually stimulating, but they often devolved into labored theological arguments. At one point, the exasperated priest pointed a finger at Jim and told him, "You know what's right. You don't need instruction. You need persuasion."

He called her "dearest" and signed most of his letters, "I love you." Sometimes he wrote it several times for good measure. What strikes me most about his letters today, what leaps off the page, is their mix of restlessness, foolishness, pretentiousness, ambition, curiosity, and sheer joy, joy that seems to have sprung from being in love with a woman to whom he could at last open his heart.

9/7/54

> *It is a deep, joyful bond. It is awakening and death—beyond the rich lore of memories of you, beyond the bleak days which proceeded. It is even beyond myself because I know it is more important to be a part of you, for us to be a part of each other, than any other thing—more important than my personality, my grubby ambitions . . .*
>
> *I shall wait to tell [the people in the bank], because it gives me so much pleasure to know it all to myself. "I love Michele." And I shall tell them, and tell my friends one by one, over a period of time, to renew the pleasure in telling about it. "I am a sleepless nothing and I know the most wonderful girl who*

*ever was and we are in love! Can you imagine such a thing?
She loves me and I love her!"*

9/20/54

*You must always take my melancholy, my despair, with a
grain of salt, for, as with all else, even when I am in it I am
removed from it. I am very much like an actor who has mas-
tered the arts of pretense—and the secret of arousing me from
my dark, gloomy thoughts is to pay no attention to them. In
some areas, I do believe I am nothing without an audience.
Perhaps at times I seek to be mothered, I don't know, but
please, please, dear, try not to be affected! You go on being your
wonderful self and don't allow me to work upon your loving
faith and devotion.*

10/1/54

*I think I am essentially very naive. And I view the world
thru curious child's eyes . . . Because of this, I learn very
slowly. I grope and falter and react and test in every way I
know any new knowledge—I assault it, just in the way a
stubborn, opinionated child assaults the outside world from
the comfort and safety of his circumstance. I give into it only
grudgingly, hesitantly, before wildly embracing it.*

*It was not always so. How many times in my youth did I
wildly embrace some little-known person or ideal or circumstance only to be harshly rebuffed? How often did my senses
scream with brief joy only to find hovering over it the deep dark
loomings of my own limitations? How slowly did I learn my first
lesson, to curb my emotions, to curb my ideas, passions, idylls?*

10/25/54

... *It has been a very lonely week-end for me, in spite of my activity. I guess it shall always be lonely away from you from now on. I feel it—I feel we are already a part of each other, and all my joys, my anxieties, my hopes and desires are only with you. I love you, love you, love.*

11/2/54

I seem to be falling more and more deeply in love with you and I thought and continue to think, "How can I love her more than I do now?" And yet it keeps growing. I am very humble, filled with joy and nothing else seems to matter a great deal. I need you so desperately and the pain in this separation is around me in everything I do. In the bank, I have become "quiet." At home, I have a yearning to be with you. On the streets, I feel a surge of excitement and a sadness, for as I wander, I pursue the glitter, the noise, the crowds and they do nothing for me. I want you.

You are such a wonderful, wonderful girl. Such a fine, lovely girl. I am so lucky, so lucky! And I shall make you happy, I pledge that. I shall! If I never accomplish another thing.

11/6/54

I have taken a bold step tonight. Afterwards, I sat a few moments bemused, wondering if this were temporary madness, wondering as to my motives. ...

... With many other kinds of thoughts, I have been having moods and thoughts which I can only describe as being reverent. I feel a profound depth to our love and approaching mar-

riage. It seems to me that God is not far away. I believe that in order for me to realize the profundity I feel, to realize on my side the fullest potentialities of our marriage, I need some succor and aid outside our marriage itself. I feel very humble and awestruck before you and yet I realize that, in order to fulfill you and myself in the way that I wish, I need some outer guide, inspiration. . . .

I have written a letter to Monseigneur Sheen care of the E. 38th St. office. I have told him I think I am ready to begin instruction but I am not sure.

I am sure this will make you very happy, but you must not say anything about it to me—except you are happy about it or dubious about it etc. It is a test. I must come back to Catholicism if I am to do so entirely on my own, entirely outside our relationship.

11/8/54

All through yesterday, many doubts came into my mind about Catholicism. And, after thinking, brooding about it (in between Conrad stories), I went to bed only to arise and get my dictionary and look up words such as: God, sin, hell, heaven, devil. I have a great many questions to ask somebody: How did the church evolve "mortal sin"? Why is what seems to me could be called an "occasion of sin" a mortal sin? Why is seeing something like "The Miracle" a mortal sin? Who, in the first place, gave the church such a right to dictate in mundane matters or intellectual matters? According to the dictionary, one definition of sin is something about a hindrance to spiritual development. I wondered if the church accepts this interpretation and, if so, why should the church assume that everyone was made for "spiritual development"? I wondered what happened before the fateful night when Christ told his disciples he would send the Holy Ghost. Where was he during the first part of creation and the first years of the earth? Does a soul come into existence when a child is born? If so, how can it be infinite? I thought of it as perhaps an unfolding, folding, out of a prostrate God, a continual movement of souls which was what made God. Per-haps the soul is not really mine or yours etc. If, as I have always thought, it is possible to kill your soul, what purpose serves hell (in which I don't believe)? If the soul is a part of God, instead of my own, how could I kill it? destroy it? It is either infinite or finite. If it is infinite it is God; if it is finite, it must die.

12/6/54

I came home with about four bundles—I enjoy carrying them and was picturing after we're married when I shall be doing the same—perhaps now and again bringing home little surprises to delight you. Everything my eye touches these days seems richer, imbued with color and vitality it never possessed for me before. All my waking and sleeping hours are pleas-ant, happy ones. I feel fulfilled. I feel a part of the earth and deep-rooted. I feel like a contented little forest animal peering about. I am living each day as it comes, with the rich knowl-edge of what the days are building towards.

12/7/54

As I was shaving this morning, I thought I must tell you, for the future, how much I am disturbed by noises at times. The reason I was thinking about it: I was shaving and I thought about the electric razor I was given a few years back, and, on the face of it, what a fine present it is for a man. I wanted to tell you, not for the near future, but for later on—after we're married and perhaps don't discuss things like this so much, but take each other for granted more: there is nothing so shattering to me as the din of an electric razor, especially in the morning. I think my sensitivity to sound is my worst and best. Smell—not so hot. See—pretty good. Touch—good, too. Taste—fair. Sound—terrific.

12/12/54

This morning, listened to: a Mormon sermon, a Christian Science sermon, an Episcopal service. I am, as always, fascinated by all religious talks. It is not the fascination of a ready convert, though, I think, but a genuine curiosity—I think an artist's curiosity. I listen for the jargon, I listen for the conception, I listen for the voice intonations, for the emotional intensity, and I am constantly contrasting, comparing, although perhaps not always with a straight face. I am especially interested in those who have been "saved" . . .

. . . It does seem to me that when a person stubbornly refuses even to think of faith, he loses not only a substantial part of life, but, through the loss of an ability to be transformed into something else, through the inflexibility before the power of conversion, slowly many of his capacities and

potentialities begin to harden and wither. This cannot be true of everyone, though, I guess, because there have been a great many men who have grown and learned and taught without this. Perhaps it is just true of certain people—like me. And, I cannot but wonder if it would be true of me if I had not had such an intense training.

1/6/55

My impulse is to get on my knees and pray as hard as I know how, but I shall not do it, for I still fear it may be only emotion at the present. And, Father Finlay, admitting my tendency in this direction, agreed coming back to the church through emotion is not to be desired. What I am now doing is humbly submitting to what he said and following the sense I got from it, even though I do not see a clear solution.

. . . Part of the trouble, of course, is the immense moral burden in me waiting to be invoked. The instant I succumb, my life shall be one ceaseless torment after another. But, as Father Finlay put it, have not my only moments of joy been God-filled moments? Or something to that effect. He was saying when I rebelled against God, I reaped only bitter fruits. I could not FEEL the force of what he was saying but it meant something to me. It always seems to me the moments when I have known the greatest joy have been with you, but I know too, that this is only relatively so. For, it is in anticipation or retrospect with you that I have the greatest joys—the moment is always less than perfect. But, he speaks of other joys and I know well enough what he means, no matter how I try to dissimulate.

1/7/55

Why is it I cannot see? . . . There seems to be no point of Catholic theology in which I am in essential disagreement. And yet, I am pretty near where I started a week ago.

I am not willing to act, to affirm. I do not believe it is lack of faith. It must be pride or stubbornness or something similar. Part of it, of course, is fear. And—fear of my human situation. For, I think I know what I must do in life (and yet, once again, if I assent, I shall be pre-occupied with problems and difficulties which Father Finlay said are to be left for saints—I should once again be too scrupulous and uncompromising about it).

I cannot but believe it is best for me, now, to be hovering continually on the threshold. The flaw in that, from a Christian point of view, is that I fail to ACT upon my knowledge. Cowardice? Perhaps. But if so, it is not cowardice in the sense of fearing anything which might be said or conspired against me or the church in life. It is just that I think I know other things about myself and it is with them I am now primarily concerned. I do seek information if by it Father Finlay means a desire and hunger to seek people out and know them. I do seek to create out of an accumulated human experience. . . .

It is all understandable to me, but alas, I do not wish to be a redeemed soul so much as I wish to be a creative artist. I still maintain there is a place for Spillane. And for the Bowery Bum. And for the murderer. While the man or soul changes, the symbols are seemingly as universal as anything to do with men. And, I cannot help it. I am interested in all life, as it is. I am not interested in redeeming or saving. Only in knowing and in transmutating into art.

1/10/55

> *. . . I do not view religion per se as dark and gloomy and filled with sin and guilts. It is just that I still believe when in this realm that I was pre-destined to be something special as regards religion and God. I believe that I was meant to fast and pray etc. I also believe that this belief is false and comes from an improper understanding of my gifts.*

1/12/55

> *I suppose the most tolerable way to regard me is as a ridiculous, pompous ass of an idealist. This is consistent with the quote from Gide I made you some months ago about men who come from where I've been. Apparently, my type of man does tend to be overly idealistic. I know it and I don't know quite what to do about it. It all seems so logical to me and it seems to work so well for me.*

At Father Finlay's urging, Jim finally wrote down his beliefs and titled the document an "Apostate's Creed." It is too long to quote entirely. I have the impression that Father Finlay, tired of arguing, simply signed off on it to get rid of the exhausting young man.

The document begins, "I believe in God" and goes on to list other things in which he believes—murder, lust, revolution, suicide, growth, tolerance, knowledge—and which come down to an assertion that humans have the essential freedom to do as they wish, with the proviso that if they turn away from God, they voluntarily commit suicide. More puzzlingly, he asserts that God "works through good as well as evil" and concludes the document as follows:

> *I believe evil is destruction: I believe good is growth. I believe in each man's right to choose the realm within which he shall live. I believe, if a man has integrity and sincerity and wisdom, his truth is in discovering what is good and what is evil within his realm. I believe if he is wise enough, he shall find God's path. I believe if he is not, other people shall learn from the example of his failure. I believe, however, it is the struggle and the fight and the seeking which are the ultimate human wisdom.*
>
> *I believe evil and good are inseparable. I believe God's "Good" embraces both. I believe God is the devil and the angel.*
>
> *I believe in God.*

He forwarded a copy to Michele. In an accompanying letter, he wrote, "Understand, I do not say I am right, although right now I believe so. I only say: If I am wrong, I have a right to be, and I shall be discovered."

FIVE

✿ ✿ ✿

My father smiles, my mother beams in the grainy photo. They are about halfway down the aisle of Saint Thomas Aquinas Chapel, on the campus of the University of Connecticut in Storrs. It is shortly before noon on January 29, 1955. Less than three dozen people are on hand; my parents have decided to limit the guest list to thirty people so they can spend most of the six hundred dollars given them by Michele's mother on sheets and pillowcases. After the brief exchange of vows, they will host a small luncheon at a nearby restaurant. My mother will walk away, she will later write, "in a happy daze, with no qualms, or indeed, any feeling at all but one of complete joy."

At her insistence, they were married by a priest. Despite the tentative rapprochement between himself and the church, Jim still considered himself a non-Catholic, though he had told Michele he would probably return once he sorted out his beliefs. That was good enough for her, but Jim could tell that the priest clearly disapproved of him.

After lunch, in midafternoon, the couple drove to the

Statler Hotel in Hartford. They checked into their room, made plans to change and go out dancing, and never made it. The next morning, they slept in before driving back to Storrs and the tiny flat Michele had rented for them.

The first months after their marriage were a happy time. Together they set out, my mother once wrote, "to create ourselves from scratch." They borrowed classical-music albums like *Don Giovanni* from the library and listened together. They shared books and articles; once they even wrote to the archdiocese for permission to read and keep works banned by the Catholic Index, including *Madame Bovary*, *A Sentimental Journey*, *Pamela,* and works of Zola, Montaigne, Gide, and Balzac. On weekend afternoons they drove along the narrow country roads through towns like Warrensville, Ashford, and Chaplin, past rambling houses and farms and under sugar-maple branches that reached over their heads. They sat up in bed late at night, talking about the future. Michele envisioned them devoting their lives to literature in a big country house, with a lot of land and eight children.

Both worked on novels. Michele left her poems and stories on Jim's pillow at night, and he read and returned them with comments in the morning. They seemed confident that one of them eventually would hit it big as a writer. They tantalized themselves by imagining what it would be like to live solely off their profits from writing. They threw themselves into domestic life. Michele experimented in the kitchen, learning to make duck a l'orange, peach kuchen, and French omelets. She insisted on taking over the responsibility for writing to his mother. Jim hung shelves and racks on the walls and set to work building her a cabinet. Ten days after the wedding, Michele wrote, "I am happy and fulfilled in every way, loving and being loved, excited by the challenge of keeping it this way . . . am feeling impossibly secure and settled and happy!"

They had very little money. On his first Monday in Connecticut, Jim walked into Society for Savings Bank in Hartford carrying a letter of reference and was hired as a teller on the spot. But his salary, even combined with the $1,540 Michele made for teaching undergraduate classes, left little extra for eating out or buying new furniture. They periodically had to borrow funds from Michele's mother.

Living in cramped quarters, they learned how much they hadn't known about each other. Michele discovered that Jim's quiet, easygoing manner sometimes masked emotional detachment. When upset, he tended to withdraw. Some nights he got home late, exhausted, wanting only to disengage and relax. He, in turn, found her mercurial moods and emotional intensity overwhelming and sometimes intimidating. From her poured a constant barrage of feelings, thoughts, opinions, ideas. Her worries that they would fall short of money or that her writing was poor built until she exploded in hysterical fits of crying. Privately, moreover, he was skeptical of her intoxicating visions of the future. She had been an only child, after all, while he knew from his childhood how difficult family life could be. But he never told her about his doubts.

Friends noticed their deep affection and the way their personalities both contrasted and intersected. Michele was brilliant and engaging but could be pretentious and sometimes talked too much. Jim was smart enough to join in a discussion of various perceptions of reality one night, and down-to-earth enough to compete in a beer-fueled belching contest the next. Though Michele claimed the center of attention, friends noticed that Jim possessed his own quiet intensity and held himself to almost impossibly high moral standards. One friend thought Jim expected himself to behave like a saint.

The couple originally planned to stay in Connecticut for two years, until Michele completed her master's degree, then choose a city to settle in and start a family. But they had been following the church-sanctioned method of "rhythm control," and Michele became pregnant a month after the wedding. A son, David, was born in November. Jim couldn't resist telling his wife, "I told you so."

With the new baby, Jim began to contemplate finding a career that he could enjoy more than banking while providing for his family and having time to write. After rejecting such possibilities as a librarian or English professor, he settled on personnel work, which he had liked in the Army and which seemed to offer immediate chances for employment and a decent salary. When Michele saw a job posting from the federal government in the newspaper, it seemed foreordained: They would move to Washington, where Michele could be near her mother, while Jim could seek a job with regular promotions and raises.

During their final months in Connecticut, Jim returned to the church. His desire to do so had been building since the wedding. Always drawn by Michele's own devotion, he had been accompanying her to mass most weeks, though not taking communion. By the spring of 1956, driven by an attraction that superseded his doubts, he was skipping lunch some days to attend mass near the bank. He told Michele that he had left the church to grow but now felt he could keep growing only if he rejoined. He had fought it for as long as he could. He set up a meeting with a priest, made a general confession, and began again to take the bread and wine every Sunday morning.

※　※　※

By the time the small family reached Washington in the spring of 1957, Michele was pregnant again. They stayed with her parents for a few weeks, then found an apartment in Takoma Park, Maryland. Jim landed a job as a personnel trainee at the Bureau of Public Roads, recruiting engineers to design the new federal highways that had recently been authorized by Congress. The starting salary was $3,670 a year. Michele found work writing scripts for the U.S. Information Agency and teaching American literature and English for foreign students at Georgetown University.

A second son, Jonathan, was born in May and almost overnight upset everything in the household. Whereas David had been a good-natured baby, this one was fussy and demanding, always seemed hungry, and lay awake crying half the night. He refused to fall asleep unless he was rocked—and woke up howling as soon as the rocking stopped. Making things worse, his behavior proved infectious: David, still only eighteen months old, turned crabbier in the face of competition.

Jim told his wife it was typical behavior for small children, but Michele, an only child, had never seen anything like it. Exhausted, frayed, she began to let her idealism about raising a large family drain away. She felt overburdened and at times even ambivalent about the new baby. For weeks she had no time to read or write. She was haunted by the two different priests who had told her in the confessional that she should forget about her artistic ambitions and devote herself to her family. Despite the progress she had been making, gradually adding to her novel and writing a few tart book reviews for small periodicals, she began to wonder whether the priests had been right, that the birth of two children so soon after her marriage proved that God did not intend her to be a writer. The thought only depressed her more.

Jim helped out some. He took baths with the boys and arose when David called out for him at night. He offered to take on some of the grocery shopping and cleaning. But he still left much of the work to her, while concentrating on his job and his own writing. And in most major decisions about the boys, he simply deferred to Michele. She brought to such matters a natural forcefulness and opinions gleaned from a shelf full of books on raising children, from Dr. Spock's guidelines to the Montessori method of education. As a mother, she set demanding and unrealistic standards for herself. She would bake for them; she would play with them; she would read to them. She would carefully monitor what they ate and how they played—all while balancing their care with her writing. Jim felt she expected too much, but he said nothing, even when the failure to achieve her high expectations deepened her disappointment in herself. Instead, he slowly began to blend into the background of their daily lives.

Even after Jonathan grew out of his infancy, Michele's exhaustion and misery sometimes grew so thick they darkened the atmosphere of the house. She yelled at the boys for fighting, accused herself of being smothered by everydayness, then castigated herself for her selfishness. She melodramatically brandished her sacrifices. She was a trapped artist, a failed writer, a bad mother. Four months after Jonathan was born, she unburdened herself in her journal late one night:

> *There is no conceivable time for me to write unless I neglect my children; I have, in my 16-hour day, no more than 1 hour in entirety to myself, and sometimes not even that. There seems to be nothing beyond the drudgery and slavery of a stupid and self-defeating daily routine, cut off from all human beings, in bondage to the dullest and meanest of servile tasks—for what? Religion seems to have no effect on me at all. I love my husband and see him dragged down into the same miserable morass. Crying has become my daily companion. Jim and I have almost no time together. No Jim, no God, no writing—is this what life is—bondage to children and them alone? For what?*

Yet her moods would swing suddenly, her desires change quickly and contradictorily. Two years after Jonathan was born, she was reveling in family life and telling Jim she wanted more children. When the boys were behaving and Jim was helping and she was finding time to write, she loved being in the kitchen and driving David to nursery school and shopping at the supermarket. She was thrilled to become pregnant again in 1960, especially when she delivered a long-awaited daughter, Sarah, that fall.

But the strains of having three children in five years were showing. Michele had given up her early dreams about family life. With them went much of her convert's enthusiasm for the church. As Sarah began to crawl, Michele concluded that she could not keep having babies if she was to pursue her career. After a long week of talks with Jim, she decided to start taking the newly available birth control pill. As an unintended side effect, and without much discussion between them, Jim and Michele quit going to church.

In her journal, Michele poured out her discontent.

> *My reason for going on contraception is that I am no longer able to believe in any operative sense. For a time, belief changed me and my life, was a genuine commitment, but for the past year, this has been less and less so. I remain locked in this selfish middle-class world, and whatever impulses I feel to break out of it come from my writing, not religion. To believe implies, among other things, "Thy will be done," and from the evidence, God's will was that I should make a holocaust of my abilities and have many children. Well, I cannot accept that, have now taken positive steps to insure this not happening, and from this refusal to accept "Thy will be done" in the Catholic framework has come everything else. . . .*

Her load eased once the boys entered preschool. But she periodically struggled with a sense of feeling trapped for the rest of her life.

※ ※ ※

Through it all, Jim tried to stay steady, keeping his life as simple and solitary as possible. Michele satisfied most of his needs for companionship. They sometimes disappeared into the bedroom in the evening and sat up talking about books with the lights on. They attended concerts and plays and watched *The 20th Century* with Walter Cronkite and *Sing Along with Mitch* with the children. They moved every year or two and enjoyed exploring the city's different neighborhoods. She teased him about his heavy snoring. On Sunday mornings Michele could usually solve all but one or two clues in the *New York Times* crossword; Jim would fill in the blanks. They fretted about losing their youthful ideals but still, I think, considered themselves exceptional. They followed currents in art and politics and occasionally went to parties where they met people like David Broder, the political reporter, and Judith Viorst, the writer. People noticed that even when the couple mingled separately, Michele's eyes always followed her husband around the room. They bought Bob Dylan albums, supported civil rights, and learned a little about good cheeses and fine wine. Even as a toddler, my brother David could recite the hierarchy in his household: "Mommy, Daddy, Kennedy, and Jesus."

Other than his wife, Jim had no close friends of his own;

his friends were her friends, and most of them were couples. He did not keep up with people from college or the Army. His hobbies were mostly solitary. He read and took walks. On Saturday morning, he listened to his record albums.

And he wrote. Some nights he came home from work and immediately went into the bedroom to write. He finally finished his novel in the spring of 1960, but over the next year it was rejected by several publishers. By the following winter, he was gloomily telling Michele that his writing ambitions had hit a wall. Privately, he was beginning to suspect that his wife was the more talented writer, and he believed she thought so, too. "I feel awful for him!" Michele wrote. "There is in Jim this flood of ideas and emotions—ready to burst out and to be truly important, only to be held back by this barrier of words. Of course, he'll keep on, but how private his universe of hopes and ambitions slowly grows!"

One of her old teachers suggested he try writing for the stage, thinking drama might play to the strengths he'd always shown for dialogue and thematic exploration while avoiding his weakness for narrative. The idea appealed to Jim, in part because he thought switching from fiction might lessen the subtle but growing rivalry between him and his wife. Throughout the 1960s, he would focus on playwriting. He joined writers' groups and became an avid follower of such playwrights as Samuel Beckett, Pirandello, and Sam Shephard. He finished his first drama in the summer of 1961 and wrote several others within a few years. A few local directors in Washington's small but growing theater community were enthusiastic, and eventually a couple of his plays were produced by experimental companies. Writing for the stage, Jim continued to explore the moral and religious questions he had been asking since adolescence and feeding in his own reading. One play explored how a husband, obsessed by his wife's rape, slowly metamorphosed into the rapist. Another focused on a Christian martyr, Franz Jagerstatter.

To his children he was a kind, well-meaning, but perpetually preoccupied figure. My sister once observed that he loved his children, but the way an astronomer loves his stars. Even when he wasn't away writing or working late at the office, he often seemed remote, sitting in the corner while his wife stage-managed the family. Periodically his childhood ulcer acted up, leaving him grimacing in pain and chugging Maalox at the dinner table. Michele sometimes accused him of settling into a premature old age. But he took criticism poorly, usually by simply withdrawing further, even though he didn't mind dishing it out in an infuriating, would-that-it-weren't-so tone. Most of his arguments with Michele ended with Jim throwing up his hands and telling her to handle things any way she wanted.

Ironically, though he had entered personnel work purely to support his family, during these years Jim found most of his rewards at the office. He was surprised at how much he enjoyed his work. He did well and rose quickly as the government expanded.

He took a job at the city government's employment office in August 1959 and within a year was named chief of employment, with an annual salary of $8,985. For the next eight years he oversaw hiring for all twenty-seven agencies reporting to Washington's mayor. He coordinated recruitment for major positions, served on the employee disciplinary board, and interviewed all major candidates.

He discovered he liked being a boss. "He has always wanted such a job, with power and authority," my mother observed in her journal after his promotion. "Now that he has it, the revelation of how much he wanted it, how richly he enjoys the work, has been a surprise, forcing him to quite thoroughly re-evaluate himself." The change was bittersweet to her. She wrote that the job would "soon provide enough satisfaction to remove further pressure from his writing. As with many of the people we talk about and analyze, Jim seems to have gone his distance."

He loved being in downtown Washington. In his first week at work, the magnolias were in bloom, and he thought he was in heaven. He had always liked the feeling of being at the center of momentous events, and Washington was filled with them in those years. One day in August 1963 he watched from his downtown office window as thousands of blacks streamed into the city from all directions and gathered on the Mall to hear Martin Luther King Jr. speak. Three months later, he was just starting a job interview when one of his employees burst into his office with the news that the president had been shot. Jim dismissed his staff, then merged into the strangely subdued throng of people who packed the buses and highways, heading home early on that eerie November afternoon.

Most of all, he liked meeting the job applicants. A steady stream of idealistic college students, poor blacks, activist ex-priests, and unwed mothers passed through his office. Remembering how he had been treated by welfare workers as a boy, he worked hard to listen to their concerns and help them find work. He considered himself an outsider in government and tried to act like an advocate for the people who came to see him, not an indifferent bureaucrat. He pushed to hire minorities and got to know some of the community leaders. He liked hiring people in trouble and helping them learn job skills and find new lives.

Meanwhile, as the children started school, Michele's career finally began to take off, too. By the midsixties she was regularly writing book reviews for *The National Catholic Reporter* and other publications. She developed a blunt, sharp-edged style, drawing upon her deep reading and finely honed intellect. She noted John Updike's propensity to "fill in the spaces with his celebrated 'fine writing,' which is quite the opposite of good writing." A book on the Holocaust served as a reminder "that the most tragic failure of Christianity is its unremitting persecution of the Jews." Reviewing James Baldwin, she praised several of his early stories but concluded that "the talent which was once so evident has been absorbed into a private fantasy which mingles sex and race, Baldwin's own guilts and fears with social problems, until the necessary honesty which is the writer's most important possession has been lost and not seen to be lost." She began to meet other writers, through letters and articles. She once interviewed the poet Joseph Brodsky and asked him what he thought of one-word poems, which were then in vogue. Brodsky sighed and told her, "I am embarrassed for the page."

A decade into their marriage, Jim and Michele were settling into a comfortable, if not wholly fulfilling, middle age. Jim grew a mustache to cover his thin upper lip, packed on a few pounds, briefly smoked a pipe before switching to Tiparillos. If their life hadn't fulfilled all the hopes of their courtship, if some of the disappointments in their writing and family life were acute, they at least remained close as friends and lovers. With some satisfaction, Michele wrote, "Our house is constantly lively, bubbling with a kind of freedom and activity and ferment that is rare, for all that the main burden rests on me . . ."

❧ ❧ ❧

In the midsixties, just as Sarah was getting ready for kindergarten, my mother suddenly decided she wanted to get pregnant one more time and stopped taking the pill. I was born on May 2, 1966.

By all accounts I was a contented, sociable baby. With age and some writing success, my mother had mellowed, and she allowed herself to be delighted with me. By the time I was walking, my parents had moved to a clattering white house with black shutters, whose entrance sat below street level on a scarily busy boulevard.

My father is the first person I remember. I was two and a half years old and had just gotten my first pair of glasses. I sat in the backseat of the car, staring at my strange new reflection in the window but feeling safe because he was driving us home.

Dad had a funny mustache and a scratchy cheek that I liked to brush my face against. In the morning I leaned against the doorway to the bathroom, watching him as he mixed his shaving cream in a mug, lathered his chin with a soft brush, then scraped its sides, leaving blobs of cream and whisker floating in the sink like meringues. He always coated himself lavishly with talcum powder, then took a swig of mouthwash, gargled elaborately, and spat it into the sink with a great splat. If I asked, he would pour me a small portion in the cap and instruct me not to swallow it. At night I lay in my pajamas on the living room rug, my feet in the air, wait- ing for one of my brothers or my sister to clap them together as I sang a little song about how happy I would be when Daddy got home. Sometimes it was so late that I only received a quick kiss from him before being shuttled off to bed; often he didn't get home in time at all. After dinner, he sat peace- fully at the head of the table, then spent five minutes carefully cleaning his teeth with a toothpick. Later, he sometimes ate pound cake and ice cream and watched *Kojak* or *Cannon* to relax.

When he was home, he felt like a big physical anchor. He was the parent who never lost his temper. Mom hated to be interrupted when she was writing and was constantly setting up a toy to occupy me so she could work for a few hours. But Dad never minded if I entered the den, waded through the haze to find him sitting in his chair, and asked him what he was doing. He brought me along when he went out to buy the papers, or to the special bakery to buy cheese danish, or to the liquor store where all the men knew his name. He presided at holiday dinners, went out for ice cream, and every few months drove us to a Chinese restaurant in Georgetown where the owner always made a big fuss over our family and I drank cup after cup of heavily sugared tea. He handed out spare change and sticks of mint gum. He talked to me seriously, as if I were a little adult. He laughed as hard as anyone when we joked about his growing bald spot and teased him as a befuddled but well-meaning blunderer who was losing his memory. When my parents took bicycle rides along the C&O Canal, I chose to sit behind him and feel his warmth. When I was five and ready for my own bicycle, he came home from work early one summer day and ran alongside me as I wobbled down the sidewalk in front of our house.

There was no question that he was not the head of our household. That was my mother, in no uncertain terms. Mom woke me up in the morning, fixed my breakfast, drove me to school, picked me up, hung my drawings on the refrigerator, fixed my SpaghettiOs, ironed my clothes in the den, knew all the answers on *Jeopardy!,* corrected my manners, spanked me, and sat at the dining room table teaching me to read with flash cards. She read to me every night before I fell asleep. Yet she could rapidly become angry or impatient and start upbraiding me for having unkempt hair or poor manners. I was always a little wary around her. My father was a steady, comforting figure. I didn't ask a lot of him. But when he was around the house, everything seemed right.

Dad was also the one who woke me early on Sunday, then drove us to church. My parents had returned, sort of, when I was about three years old. My mother had been feeling some old longings for mass, and the fallout from Vatican II, which nurtured a host of grass-roots experiments meant to make the mass more "relevant" to Catholics, offered an unexpected array of choices. Mom discovered a group that met for weekly services in a high school cafeteria in northern Virginia and punningly called itself Nova.

My parents felt at home in Nova. They found there a few hundred people whose backgrounds and aspirations were similar to their own, most of them middle-class couples with children and creative leanings. There was no rigid hierarchy dictating proper procedures. Members rotated the planning of liturgies among themselves. Each week the organizers selected the readings and music, invited a priest to preside, and baked fresh bread and selected wine. Everything was served in earthy wooden bowls. Folk guitarists led us through the service, culminating in a swinging "Amen" chorus before the Eucharist. The programs could be incredibly complicated; members sometimes wrote long dialogues between the priest and the congregation, or inserted poems or films they thought would illuminate the weekly message. My father once adapted a Tolstoy story, "Where Love Is, There God Is," for use in a service.

It's easy for me to make fun of Nova today, but I loved it when I was small. The people were friendly and the music was joyous. I sat in the backseat of the car on the way home, listening to my parents talk about Jesus and God and feeling that they were very close. I pictured God as a cartoonish old man, a peaceful figure with a curlicue beard, a shy smile, and eyes contentedly closed tight beneath a Jimmy Durante hat.

My parents became so comfortable at Nova that they decided to have my long-delayed baptism there one Sunday when I was five years old. I wore a little red swimsuit. I scampered to the front of the room, jumped into a wading pool, and raced back to my seat as fast as I could. I was embarrassed because I knew that people were usually baptized when they were babies, and I didn't want anyone in the room to think I was little. I hid my face in my towel when the congregation broke into applause.

* * *

In the summer of 1969 my mother took the children to England for a long vacation. Dad stayed home, alone, so he could finish a play he had been working on and start a new job he'd taken as personnel director for the sanitary engineering department.

But only a few days after we left, he got a phone call from a man named Jerry Wilson, who had just been named chief of police in the city. He was planning a major overhaul of the department and told Dad that he expected most of the problems he would face in the first year to be personnel-related. He wanted Dad to come work for the police as director of personnel.

Dad was flattered, but at first he balked. He told Jerry he couldn't leave a job he'd just started and abandon his newly handpicked staff. But Jerry pressured him. To win Dad his freedom, he interceded with the mayor, and within a week Dad found himself at his first press conference, fielding questions about his record and laying out an ambitious agenda for overhauling the force.

Wilson's mandate was modernization. He wanted more women and minorities, more college graduates, and a new, professionalized personnel system through which to steer his officers. Washington lagged other cities in benefits and training procedures. In a haze of red tape, officers and civilians reported to separate chains of command and advanced through the buddy system. Wilson wanted to unite them under one, uniform standard. Most important, he intended to expand the force by several thousand officers. The city had just received a grant under President Nixon's "law and order" program, and most of it was devoted to recruitment and training.

"It was a matter of getting in someone who had had some expertise," Wilson, now in his seventies and retired, told me when I called him up at his home in rural Maryland. "We were trying to update the personnel climate to match the rest of the government. I wanted a personnel specialist."

In this setting, Dad was the ultimate outsider: a high-ranking civilian in a veteran police department, a reformer in a bastion of conservatism, a liberal sympathetic to minorities in what was still a very white, Southern force of four thousand officers. "He was probably the highest-ranking civilian at a police agency in America," Paul Fuqua, who was then the public information officer for the department, told me.

My father worked for the department for more than four years and considered it the best job he ever had. Almost overnight he was working six days a week and sometimes twenty hours a day. The politically charged atmosphere and public scrutiny were like nothing he had experienced before. The department was a nexus for virtually every major public issue of the day: civil rights protests, welfare debates, anti-war demonstrations, and rising crime. Little over a year earlier, dozens of blocks had been looted and burned during the riots that broke out after the assassination of Martin Luther King Jr. Inside and outside the ranks there was fear that Washington would explode again. At a time when the city's population was only about 30 percent white, three fourths of the force was. Black citizens often refused to cooperate with police; many referred to the department as an "army of occupation." Jerry Wilson told Dad he had to increase that percentage quickly. "We were at the center of the universe at that time," Paul Fuqua told me. "We were a front-page story every day."

Dad received calls from reporters and subpoenas from congressional committees. He gave occasional TV interviews and became a frequent radio guest. With his long hair and sideburns, pastel shirts, and wide ties—selected by my mother—he stuck out conspicuously. One newspaper dubbed him "the Mod Cop." "The cops even placed a good deal on appearance, and Jim certainly didn't look like a cop," recalled Donald Graham, publisher of the *Washington Post,* who was then a patrolman in the department. In cloistered Washington, he became a minor celebrity. Nationally, his profile soared as word spread of his efforts to remake the force.

The changes were sweeping and rapid. Within Dad's first fifteen months, the police hired close to two thousand new officers, nearly half of whom were black. Female officers joined street patrols for the first time. Dad united the uniformed and civilian personnel structures and revamped the department's disciplinary board. He personally interviewed every employee, uniformed or not, recommended for dissmisal during his probation period.

When he disagreed with the commanding officers recommendation, he would recommend to the chief that the employee not be fired. Chief Wilson almost always backed my father. Dad tried to bring to the job the same qualities he had always employed—primarily, an ability to listen and respectfulness. "He always had a spiritual side he didn't hide the way many bureaucrats would," said Mary Ellen Abrecht, who was an officer in the department then and later became a judge in the D.C. superior court. She surprised me by saying she wasn't surprised to hear of his later vocation as a monk.

At the office, Dad showed that you didn't need to have a uniform to win trust—or power. Anomalous as he was, he quickly became part of the closed inner circle surrounding Wilson, a tall, imposing man with an ingratiating drawl and laid-back manner. Dad was one of a handful of senior officials who could pick up the phone and reach Chief Wilson instantly, access he used to carve out a unique role for himself. "He intellectualized," Fuqua told me. "He could sit at a table and come up with suggestions that I don't think would come from other folks. It doesn't mean they were always good, but Jerry was able to sit back and say, 'Roy, what do you think of this?' 'Bill, what do you think about that?'"

Several years after Dad started, Wilson even contemplated

making him one of four uniformed assistant chiefs, despite his civilian status. After Dad told him he didn't want a uniform, Wilson compromised by giving him the duties and trappings of the job but fudging the title slightly. He pressured him into signing out the unmarked police car that went to the assistant chief and defended him after officers "objected that it was unprecedented power for a civilian." Soon Dad was invited to visit departments in other cities to lead workshops on the techniques he had used to reshape the personnel system in Washington, with particular emphasis on recruiting. He also was asked to join a task force on the matter organized by the Justice Department.

But he faced a constant backlash. Almost immediately, veteran officers had begun complaining about the power and growing prestige of this nonuniformed newcomer. Dad tried to win support where he could; he once stood before hundreds of officers at a luncheon, told them he empathized with the stresses they faced, and invited them to come see him if they needed anything. A few did, but others took early retirement to escape the changes in the department. "They hated his guts," Paul Fuqua told me. "It was brutal on him. Whenever some of the mossbacks could screw him, they would." During his first year on the job, Dad was hauled before three separate congressional subcommittees and asked to explain what he was doing. Sometimes he was almost devious in response. When officers complained to the city's oversight committees that a civilian had been handed personnel oversight and was hiring unqualified men without the input of uniformed cops, Dad and Jerry Wilson created a plan to rotate sergeants into his office for stints of two or three months. The idea was to give the rank and file input but prevent anyone else from building a power base in the personnel office.

Among other initiatives, they took heat for their efforts to recruit college graduates. Because most of them could be expected to stay only a few years, the city had traditionally looked elsewhere for career officers. Veterans often viewed graduates with suspicion and distrust. But Wilson, who was then a twenty-year veteran himself, told Dad to ignore the informal ban. "There was a philosophy in the department that you should only hire people who wanted to be police officers, which is a crock," Wilson told me. "People who *want* to be police officers, well, I'm afraid of them myself. Most officers are like me: They took the job because it was a job they could get. My idea was that if you got a college recruit who came in and stayed for three or four years, so what? It cost a little to train them, but I figured it would be good because then lots of people out there who were doctors and lawyers would know what the police force was like."

I don't want to overstate my father's achievements. In the highly charged environment, Dad made some mistakes. One man he hired in his office turned around and hired one of his girlfriends. When Dad confronted him, he denied the relationship, but officers from internal affairs learned the mistress was illegally collecting welfare checks even after she had been hired. Dad wasn't even notified of the investigation until after they were arrested one weekend. Another time, the *Washington Post* reported that the police had hired our family's landlord—and that shortly afterward our security deposit was returned. Dad insisted that the two events were unrelated, but he didn't come off well in the article. Incensed, he told his boss he wanted to write a letter, but Wilson just laughed and told him, "Jim, my experience is that if you get publicity, people are gonna take shots at you. It'll go away in a day or two—unless you speak up about it."

The long-term benefit of his work in Washington has been debated for twenty-five years, especially since the police started to get bogged down in the city's soaring crime rate during the 1980s. Donald Graham told me, "They ended up with a far better department than the one your Dad came to." Another ex-officer, James Lardner, who later became a writer specializing in police matters, told me my father radically reshaped the force through the influx of new recruits and departure of old-timers. "There was an opportunity to change the department faster than just about has ever happened with a police department," he said. "Jerry Wilson and Jim Murray were a pretty terrific team."

But Paul Fuqua told me he thought the overall effect was minimal. "Did we make a major impact on American policing?" he said. "No. I don't think reform did anything. What your father and Jerry did was keep the department from blowing up at a time when everyone thought it might. They kept it under control. They were tough guys."

※   ※   ※

Dad quit the department at the end of 1973. He felt burned-out and didn't want to stick around beyond the expected departure of Jerry Wilson. By the time he left, the force was nearly 40 percent black and more than 25 percent larger. He had recruited almost half of the current officers.

If he had felt any frustration from his job, it came not at work but from my mother's seeming ambivalence about it. She told him she was excited for him, joined him at parties and public events, and worried about his safety. Yet between his job and her writing, they started to grow apart. She often was too absorbed in her work to listen to him talk about his. She no longer left poems on his pillow or clipped articles for him to read. The old connection through literature had faded. Years later, reading her journals after her death, he was dismayed to see that she never wrote about his job, except to complain about his long hours. "Jim is still working all the time," she wrote in February 1970. "Pas marriage."

He nonetheless left with great satisfaction over his record. Frustrated with his writing, feeling stuck in a middle-class morass, he had unexpectedly found a role in which he could influence people's lives and receive some public attention. He had reveled in the long hours and political infighting. Despite a late start, he had reached the pinnacle of his profession.

Yet the satisfactions were tempered, darkened slightly by other, usually unstated, concerns. For all the pleasures he felt in throwing himself into the job, my father's drive, and my mother's frustrations, reflected personal pressures with which both were quietly grappling. They weren't discussed much. But both knew, during those years, that an inescapable cloud loomed.

S I X

❊ ❊ ❊

"The world *is* real and the flesh takes its revenge."
—FROM MY MOTHER'S JOURNAL, AUGUST 28, 1968

It was odd to find Steve's mother pacing on the sidewalk as we came out of school on that mild Thursday in mid-March. Odder still, she said she was there to take me and Steve back to their house.

Steve, who at nine was nearly a year and a half older than me, had been my best friend since the day I started at my new school the year before. I had stood nervously at the front of the second-grade classroom while Mrs. Allen introduced me and asked whether anyone would volunteer to sit next to me. Steve leapt from his seat. We were pals by lunchtime.

We had since fallen into a pattern of playing together nearly every afternoon, usually at my house. We could walk there in five minutes. My house was preferable to his, because of an atmosphere of controlled chaos that two boys found highly stimulating. There were piles of old newspapers scattered around the floor, barking dogs and mewling cats, clacking type-

writers, blaring televisions and record players, unmonitored
telephones on which to make crank calls in funny Chinese
voices, the pleasant rip of fresh bags of cookies and potato
chips being opened, prickly brothers and a thin-skinned sister
to be ridiculed. There was a window well next door where we
often found toads. There was a wide, unfenced backyard where
we could run through the sprinklers on hot afternoons, then a
grove of bamboo trees whose thick, hard stalks we could bend
over and break off with awesome strength when we felt like
metamorphosing into our secret superhero alter egos. Beyond
the bamboo lay several hundred yards of woods, and on the
other side of those was Rock Creek Park, where we could ride
our bicycles along the gravel path, hunt for turtles, or simply
launch an empty plastic Cool Whip container into the creek
and race along the banks, watching as the current carried it
along.

If there was any disadvantage to my house, it was my
mother. She didn't like Steve much. He was a little too fresh
and daring for her taste. She thought he would get me into
trouble. But as long as we kept quiet and out of her way, she
left us alone. One of the advantages of the suburbs was that
we could roam about pretty freely. She didn't need to watch
us every second. We just had to be home by dark. Sometimes
we didn't see any parents all afternoon.

Yet here was Steve's mom, speaking in a soft voice and
seeming a bit preoccupied. She said my father had called and
asked her to pick me up and bring me to their house to play.
I was a little surprised but didn't give it too much thought. I
did what I was told.

At about five-thirty, with the sun just beginning to fade overhead, Steve's mom came into the backyard to tell me my father was on his way over. She helped me on with my jacket and suggested I wait out front. She seemed more careworn than before, and almost a little glad to get rid of me.

Dad pulled up a couple of minutes later. As we pulled away from the curb, he was silent.

He now had a drive of about four minutes before him: to the end of the block, a right turn, three more blocks, another right, then straight up the road to our house. I stared out the window.

"How was your day?" he asked at last.

"Fine."

"Did you have fun at Stephen's?" He sounded a bit nervous.

"Yep."

"Good."

From the backseat, I could see in the rearview mirror that his eyes were fixed on me. "Matthew, I have something to tell you," he finally said. "Your mother died this afternoon, at about one o'clock."

She had died peacefully, he said. Sarah and Jonathan and David were already home and knew what had happened. A few of my parents' friends were over at our house, too.

"Do you understand what dead is?"

I did.

"Is there anything you want to ask me?"

I thought for a minute. Slightly stunned, I didn't really want to say anything. I could tell that he didn't want to say anything else either now that the horrible news was out. I looked out the window and suddenly felt surrounded by mystery and loss and curiosity and the realization that fears I had not fully understood had come true. So I just sat there, thinking over and over: *dead dead dead,* determined not to be a baby who would cry, determined to show that I could be all right, a little stoic who was baffled and sad and numb and a little scared by the idea that someone could just be there, then not be there.

We said nothing during the last minute or two of the drive. He parked in front of our house and went inside, and I saw my brothers and sister sitting in the living room with stone faces while pairs of adult legs swirled around me. I joined the rest of them. We were supposed to sit. Someone had made us a spaghetti dinner, but no one was very hungry.

Later that night, my father invited each of us to go into my mother's den and remove any knickknack we wanted from her desk, a paperweight or a desk calendar or something, just to claim an object that had been hers as recently as that morning. It seemed very important to him to orchestrate a little ritual that would involve us in her death. I walked into the dark room and chose an ugly little blue-and-yellow ceramic angel, which I had bought her for Christmas three months earlier. It still sits on my bookshelf today.

But I don't remember much else from that evening, except for the unsettling feeling of the world rotating around us while we five sat, huddled, stuck in silent, suspended animation.

Even to a seven-year-old, the news was not a complete surprise. My mother had been dying for a long, long time.

In July 1968, when I was two years old and my mother was thirty-five and the older kids were finally all off at school and she had a little extra time to herself, she felt a welt on her breast during a difficult, restless night. The next morning, a Friday, she went to the doctor. He immediately checked her into the hospital. On Monday he removed her breast. The next week, she underwent a hysterectomy.

Typically, one of my mother's first acts in the midst of this sudden crisis was to begin a new journal. "Well, all my growing secret fears—of this summer, or my whole life, I suppose—are out in the open now," she wrote after her first diagnosis, on July 27, 1968.

It is not only the operation—which will be bad enough and finish me as I was—it is that more and more I believe that the doctor will do nothing because it will be too late and I am riddled with cancer and dying, leaving all these children . . . All this for no reason, no meaning, absolutely no purpose. At best, my life broken. At worst, my suspicions, a wretched death at 35—just like that, when my poems and translations are coming to fulfillment, when my children's book will probably be accepted—all too late. I have always been most afraid of living and dying like a grain of sand on a beach, accomplishing nothing, and so it will be. I am not surprised but stunned and terrified. I am nothing of a heroine, not brave, and I did not want this—yet why have I always suspected that I would be asked to pay for all I have? At the same time, what good my gifts if they demand my life? I expect nothing more, there will be nothing but a painful end.

After her hysterectomy, the doctor told my father he had found cancer in thirty of her thirty-two lymph nodes. We couldn't get it all, he said. My father later learned that the doctor believed she had only six more months to live.

Dad had promised before the operation to be frank with my mother if she inquired about her outlook. But when he went in to see her, she didn't even need to ask. She guessed the answer by the look on his face and started screaming and crying before he could get any words out. Dad had to summon the doctor to help calm her down.

As it turned out, she had more than five years to live. And as she recovered and tried to resume something resembling a normal life, it became clear to everyone that the illness had transformed her.

You could see it in her work. She had previously been a little scattershot and undisciplined; now she became more focused and selfish about carving out blocks of time. She wrote furiously, almost ruthlessly, with a depth and passion she had not previously demonstrated. In the next five years, she completed two children's books, edited an anthology of writings about women, and wrote enough poems to fill a fourth book as well as numerous essays, reviews, and articles. She started contributing to better-known and better-paying publications like the *Washington Post* and *The New Republic*. She wrote a few freelance reviews for the *National Observer,* a weekly newspaper, that so impressed the arts editor there that he asked her to become his book editor. This provided her, for the first time in her writing life, with an office to which she could escape several mornings a week.

As her reputation grew, she cultivated ties in the literary world with writers like Tillie Olsen and Marge Piercy. With my father's profile also rising because of his police work, they began to attract some of the attention they had long desired. They attended more parties and widened their circle of friends. They gave a few newspaper and magazine interviews. They bought a new house and their first new car.

In her personal relationships, my mother displayed a new-found sympathy for ordinary people who suffered, people like my father's mother, on whom she had once looked down. Her old intellectual arrogance began to subside.

And she pushed herself wherever she could. She learned to bake bread and made her first four-layer cake from scratch. She fought with David, convinced she could prod him out of a difficult adolescence. She gathered the whole family together for outings to a Greek restaurant and the ballet and the premiere of the movie *Fiddler on the Roof.* She took French classes but never made much progress. She bought a trendy Chinese cookbook and learned to use a wok.

Feeling she lived under a death sentence, she planned a ten-week trip to England for the children and tried to forget about the expense. For all her reading and romantic longing, she had never been overseas before. She traveled to London, Bath, Swanage, and Stonehenge but grew tired easily, worried about money, disliked the English tourists, and felt worn down by the children. She missed my father greatly, especially as she grew anxious about his new job. "It is bound to change our lives, especially his," she wrote. "Does he secretly suspect that the die has been cast?" In August she decided to cut the trip short and fly home.

She remained self-critical, sometimes harshly so. She watched her figure disappear, cursed her body for betraying her, and complained that she felt like a woman in her late fifties, not her late thirties. In her journal, she compiled a list of the things she didn't do enough but wanted to:

> *laugh freely*
> *remember my dreams*
> *just walk*
> *spend the day out of the house*
> *entertain*
> *relax*
> *take time for nothing*
> *respond freshly to the children*
> *have enough sex*
> *pray and meditate*
> *yoga*
> *enough bike riding*

In some ways she began to outgrow my father. Her literary success now outstripped anything he had achieved as a writer. While Dad got wrapped up in his job, she increasingly turned for companionship to her new writing friends and colleagues.

This is not to say they did not stay close. When Dad was

home in the evening he tried to help with the housework so she could write. They still disappeared into their room for late-night talks and rode their bicycles along the canal on Sundays. Dad tried to please her and let her know he loved her. And he tried as hard as he could to forget that at any moment everything would be unalterably and forever changed.

❊   ❊   ❊

Five years after her first diagnosis, my mother went in for a routine checkup and was found to be remarkably cancer-free. The doctor did suggest removing her remaining breast, purely as a precaution against a recurrence, but she talked it over with my father and decided against it.

A few weeks later, Mom went outside one afternoon to trim our unwieldy front bushes with a new electric hedge trimmer. As soon as she turned it on, waves of unpleasant vibrations ricocheted through her body. She could barely hang on to the tool. In bed that night, she was racked with pain and unable to sleep.

Just to be safe, she returned to the doctor. This time they found the cancer. And that fall it moved into all of our lives with a stunning and unexpected swiftness.

After examining her, the doctor urged my mother to have her adrenal glands removed. He hoped the operation would produce another remission. She agreed, but it failed to help. Instead, two days after surgery, she lay in her hospital bed on a Sunday afternoon, pale, sickly, breathing shallow breaths while her mother and husband sat by her bed. She looked like she was dying, but when Dad called the nurses, they assured him she was fine. With a growing sense of unease, he finally pushed them to summon the doctor from his home. When he arrived, he quickly examined her, then spent the next two hours injecting needles and pumping things into her. Once she was stable, he told my father she had indeed been close to death when he arrived.

That crisis established a pattern that dominated the next six months. On the surface we led a life of placidity. Without saying anything, we all tacitly agreed to live as normally as possible. But our days were punctuated by moments of unexpected terror. One day my father was standing on a ladder painting the living room ceiling when he heard my mother walk into the room and say, "Jim." He looked down to see bloody strands of mucus streaming from her nostrils. Paint-spattered, he dropped everything to rush her to the hospital.

By midwinter, the cancer had spread to her bone marrow. She lost weight. Her hair fell out. She worked as often as she could, but bursts of creative energy alternated with bouts of intense pain. Sometimes she would wake in the night, needing to use the bathroom, and it would take hours for her to muster the strength to sit up, then stand, then walk across the hall. Other nights she gave up trying to sleep altogether and sat up listening to classical music on the phonograph.

Around that time, my parents were interviewed by *Washingtonian* magazine for an article on twelve "supercreative" Washingtonians. The piece focused on area artists and included a profile of my father. He was portrayed as a dynamic bureaucrat who busted red tape during the day and crafted plays at night. In the forefront of the photo accompanying the article, he casually leaned back in his office chair, confident, happy, healthy, longish hair swept to the side, a friendly smile on his face, a man in the prime of his life. On the couch behind him, a little out of focus, sat my mother, looking like an old woman: bent, thin, about to break.

Asked by the writer what he wanted to do with his life, my father said he hoped he could eventually write full-time and "become a wise old man."

* * *

During her final illness, my mother returned with new diligence to the journal she had been keeping for nearly twenty-five years. In her careful handwriting, she recorded the progression of her illness, setting the cold mechanics of her treatment alongside her own reflections:

> *September 17, 1973: Beginning of the final stage for me, known and predicted five years ago and now being played out—exactly how not known, but the result not in doubt. How stupid it is! I had always anticipated middle age, not youth, as the best part of my life and work, and here I am 40—facing an unpretty, lingering death within five years. And it's all totally out of my control—me, who likes so much to be in control! I am not especially angry or frightened—yet—only curiously calm and alienated from what is happening, fighting to separate the me from the body it is in.*
>
> *It could be said that all my cleverness and intellectual*

activity was a way of compensating for, and drawing attention away from, a body that was only a disgrace and an
embarrassment ... Even after 18 years with Jim, I find I
turn away from sex because I hate to have him see my body. I
think more and more that he is pretending in all that he says
and is only waiting for me to die so that he can marry
again—someone who is attractive and not just pretending.

It shouldn't be. I've had a hard life and I deserve time to
see the children grow up and take their places in the world—
I'd like that—as well as have some time with Jim when we
have a little money and can enjoy our time together—we never
had that, since David was born 10 months after we were married. And I need time for my poetry, since I'm coming into
my own very slowly. That's one thing I couldn't rush even
though I could rush through school and children. There should
be time for this—and there won't be and nothing will replace
that.

When I think of the poetry, I get most depressed—this is
what I was born to do—and now ...

Four days in the hospital. I can read and write reviews but
poetry is impossible here—and there will be more hospital in
my future. Nothing helps. Except to think of others—a little.

September 18, 1973: Liver scan, bone marrow, skull
X-ray. Exhaustion. All the doctors repeat that my anemia is
severe. When I was weighed Sunday on the hospital scale it
was 134, tonight 129. Naturally, my imagination runs
wild—do they anticipate lesions in the skull or brain? Or is it
just routine precaution?

September 26, 1973: More pain than I could have believed possible.

September 29, 1973: I wouldn't have been able to imagine so much pain—from the removal of the anesthesiology equipment from my throat and mouth to the present rib and incision pain. And more to come. Sores from all the shots. Blood and IV drips. Swollen mouth, gas pains, not enough water. Unable to sit up, turn over, roll over. No appetite. Foul-tasting mouth. Muscle pain. Bruised buttocks. Ugliness. Distended belly. Dried skin, mottled and aged. And never-ending pain. The body not a friend but an enemy that must be yielded to.

October 2, 1973: Still weak after a bad setback on Sunday—physical and psychological—great pain from gas, blood count dropping, not enough cortisone, and I am so tired, so very tired. I don't want to fight anymore. I want to die. I am going to die, there is nothing but pain and it will be over, I can't open my eyes, people are doing things to me and I don't care . . . yet I'm here two days later, much better, pulled back into life—skill, love, two days of tubes and blood and drugs . . . and mystery.

Like grains of wheat shaken out of the hand—melting wheat—like winnowing sacks of rice.

October 4, 1973: Low day. Cortisone dosage cut and I felt physically tired, dispirited, emotionally dead. For someone like me, who has been able to control, it is painfully hard to accept that it is no longer in my control. I must go along with these physical tides. It is terrifying to have to give up so much— and to have to. No hope of choice. In the long run, it may be a spiritual and artistic blessing, but living through days like this without falling apart will be hell. And many of them.

October 16, 1973: Pain—if I can keep the Darvon going around the clock, with aspirin at bedtime and in the morning, the pain is tolerable and occasionally even goes away, leaving only stiffness and aches. Otherwise, the pain is constant and sometimes incapacitating, especially in one place on my back.

October 22, 1973: In to work today and feeling good and then, just as I walked out the door, Jim Andrews of Sheed & Ward called to say that they were going to publish my poems! I didn't talk to him about anything else because I was so excited. So that's the tradeoff—my life for my poems. And didn't I always secretly know it all these calm and ripening years?

November 15, 1973: I don't want to die, so I manage to adjust myself to the life that I must lead and to do it in such a way that no one thinks of me as an invalid. But why am I still so tired? And why this continuing back pain? Well, it's in one spot only, but it is severe—when I don't take any Empirin, I can't move and the Darvon doesn't work. Today I dozed from 9 to 10 and from 1 to 2. It is a paradise outside—warm and sunny with crisp leaves on the ground and I cannot walk easily enough to go outside and be in this day. . . . I would like to—it is alive outside.

Curiously enough, I do not resent this enforced quiet—the first in my life, really, but sink into it, accept it. All around, public life is crumbling, too, yet in the end the note continues to be joy.

November 30, 1973: All of a sudden, everything has changed dramatically for the worst, and I'm at the end. Three, six, nine months is the story and I wonder if I'll be alive to see my poems published; probably not, if Jim Andrews doesn't send them along soon. And I've got to make arrangements for the second book of poems—retyping and editing—redo my will, try to finish Dacia's War—*but how?—and leave letters to Jim and the children. Sort out my reviews, clip them and bundle them. All the while being tired and in pain.*

December 5, 1973: Nothing will be possible. It is only a matter of time. I won't see my poems published or my book finished or the second book underway. Even my handwriting is that of a dying person. All I want to do is sleep and die.

December 8, 1973: They have turned me into a thing, not a person. I am finished living, no matter what happens.

December 13, 1973: . . . My poor Jim, who has been so marvelous, is tired, more and more tired every day, after handling so much on his own since August—more and more, through the fall and winter—and now he's giving out as well. Fortunately, he'll have two successive four-day weekends in a row at Christmas and New Year's and possibly I'll be in some shape to help by then. A very quiet Christmas.

No matter what anyone says, in some ways the single clear death would have been easier once it was all over. It is life that is hard and dying that is even harder but death that is very easy and complete.

Dear God, help me to try with all that is in me to help Jim as he has helped me—no one has ever been so marvelous to another person—and I don't deserve it.

December 24, 1973: Last evening was transcendent. Bob celebrated a liturgy here for us and the Hunts, Joan and her mother, Doris and her friend . . . and it was for me a true healing experience, the center of our holiday. The dinner that Jim made according to my directions was delicious, and today has been mainly quiet, everyone happy with gifts, a small, tranquil Christmas. I could have been in the hospital! More than anything else, I'm overwhelmed by the feelings I seem to have evoked in other people—impossible to believe, stunning me.

December 30, 1973: Better by far since Thursday morning, readying myself for Dr. Alpert's decision on Thursday, because I'll be sick again once the chemotherapy starts. What this better means is that I am now functioning, with a good deal of pain, at approximately 1/4 to 1/3 of my lowest level before—very depressing. Almost nothing interests me—shellshock—no ideas, no response to most books, no sense of being part of life again, of being involved in the ongoing activities of normal people. If this doesn't return, nothing else will be

worthwhile, yet I am at the mercy of the purely physical trans-
formations wrought by all these drugs. I feel trapped and can't
even express it because I must play the invalid's part, which
doesn't include rage. I think I am still more inclined to death
than to life, and the reversal will involve a long-time effort.
Why bother? At the very best I'll never have much to offer
again. My brain is foggy, everything disappears into mists . . .

January 16, 1974: Continuing diminishment, and rather
rapidly, really. I think it would be entirely correct to say that I
am dying, whether the process takes six months or two years.

February 1, 1974: Last Sunday my nose bleeds finally got
the better of me and one of them wouldn't stop but turned
into a hemorrhage that ran down my throat and almost choked
me. We called the doctor because I knew I couldn't lose much
blood—I was already very sleepy and pale—and he told us to
go to Suburban Hospital and get my nose packed, which I
did. Then they did blood tests and decided I needed more
blood and had to get it at GW, so a BCC Rescue Squad ambu-
lance took me off and there I was in the hospital again and
bitterly regretting the whole thing.

Wretched night. No sleep—nose still packed, could breathe
only through mouth and hooked up to IV and blood—at 1 A.M.
and at 4 A.M.—couldn't move, couldn't breathe. No radio.
Bored. Nose unpacked at 1:30 A.M. Ugh! More blood at 1:45,
not unhooked until 4:15 after getting my cytoxin, then home
with Jim after work. Weird interlude! Feel much better now,
though, with all that blood, am really having good days, except

for more back pain and still nose bleeds. Saw nose doctor yesterday and go again in a week. Ridiculous. I'll never be more than a semi-invalid after all of this.

February 13, 1974: Need more blood tomorrow—2 units—after only a bit more than 2 weeks—so I imagine the chemotherapy treatments will stop soon. Meanwhile, my hair is just about gone and has been coming out in handfuls. I wear a wig. My nails have broken to the quick, and the pads of my fingers are all cut and cracked and scored—more results of the treatment—and I continue to feel quite good, even though physical activity exhausts me.

March 9, 1974, 4 A.M.: Perhaps I am dying right now. Curious symptoms—lightness of spirit, numbness of extremities, heart flutters, joy.

❈ ❈ ❈

From her last days, I retain only the uneasy feeling of things not being themselves. It was less than two months before my eighth birthday, and consciously or not, I wasn't paying much attention to my immediate surroundings. I don't even remember whether I saw her in the last six weeks of her life. I can't summon up a single image of her when she was very sick. She never said good-bye to me. She just vanished into the den, a cold room at the end of a long hall in the back of the house. No one told me not to go back there, but I knew to stay away. Mom had to rest. Though she met with each of the other children in the days before she died, my father told me years later that she didn't want me carrying some awful memory of her wasted frame and frail limbs and bald head for the rest of my life.

I had never spent as much time around my father as I did in those days. He was suddenly home all the time, if more distant and distracted than usual, trying to fix the meals and do the dishes and pick up the dry cleaning and take Mom to the doctor. The days rearranged themselves into new patterns; my father started to pour my cereal in the morning and pick my coat up off the floor where I left it in the afternoon.

Late at night, after I was in bed, my mother and father would talk about her life, about what she had achieved, about what would become of him after she died. He told her he loved her. She told him he would have a hard time finding another woman to marry after she died. She said she had loved being his wife and a mother, and that she had never appreciated those things enough until the end.

One Monday morning in late winter, my mother got up, drove to her office, and handed in a review of a book by Annie Dillard called *Pilgrim at Tinker Creek*. She sat down at her desk intending to get to work but suddenly had an onset of double vision. A coworker had to drive her home. Frantic, she telephoned her chemotherapist. The doctor, much calmer than she was, suggested she try changing the dosages of her medication and give it a day or two. He seemed to think it was less serious than she did; my mother, after all, could get hysterical when scared. If the symptoms persisted, he said, she should go to the hospital for tests. He recommended that Dad reserve a private ambulance as a standby measure. But she turned out to be sicker than the doctor suspected.

On Tuesday night, she wrote in her journal: "If someone were to say to me point blank, 'Are you dying?' I'd have to say, 'Yes. And soon.' My eyes are darkening, the pain is mastering me, health has lost its battle with illness on every front . . . and the cancer advances faster than the treatment, itself lethal, can cope. My work remains, still interesting, but it must fight against pain and sleepiness. It will all be over soon."

On Thursday morning she woke up feeling as good as she had in weeks. But she was tired again a few minutes later. Dad carried her to the den to lie down. She stretched out on the couch and covered herself with a blanket. He sat by her side.

She fell asleep for a while, stirred, then slept again. A few hours passed. Coldness crept up from her fingertips. Her face started to grow rigid. After a while, my father realized she was dying.

What could he do? By this time, there didn't seem to be much. The ambulance he had reserved several days earlier was due shortly, anyway. He concluded that the best thing to do was comfort her.

Before long, they seemed to have entered a strange dreamland. She was calm. He was peaceful. The only jarring note was our dachshund, Samson, who refused to budge from the floor by her bed, where he lay whimpering. As she drifted in and out of consciousness, Dad played some Mahler and Bach on the stereo. He sat by her bed and read to her from Psalm 104:

"How varied are your works, Lord! In wisdom you have wrought them all; the earth is full of your creatures. Look at the sea, great and wide! It teems with countless beings, living things both large and small."

In the middle of the morning, the doorbell rang. A delivery man had brought a long-awaited fur coat she had ordered from Alaska. Dad carried it back to the den. He held her hand and talked to her. He told her again that he loved her. He prayed for her. For the first time since Monday, she seemed free of pain. His prevailing mood was that he had done everything he could for her, and this was part of the natural sequence of events. He had never been close to someone who was dying, and he was awestruck by the process. There were many aspects of it, like the dog's instinctive sorrow, that were beyond anything he'd ever seen before.

Just after twelve-thirty, the phone rang. It was a friend of my mother's who had had a horrible premonition and seemed very upset. Her tone shook my father. He told her what was happening, and she insisted he call for help right away. He dialed the rescue squad.

My mother died just before they got there, at about 12:50 on March 14, 1974. When the rescue workers arrived, they regarded the body on the couch and my father with suspicion. One of them pulled a sheet up over her face, and Dad pulled it back down. They tried to take her body, but he insisted that they leave it. As soon as they had gone, he called a priest and asked him to come administer the last rites. He called her doctor, who was crushed to learn what had happened. He called another friend to ask him to arrange a cremation. Friends called other friends, and soon people just started showing up at the door.

My brother Jonathan was the first one of us home. As he came up the street, he saw the priest's sedan out front and knew. Inside, he found nearly a dozen people already gathered, and a youngish priest with sandy brown hair whom he had never met. Dad seemed fairly calm when he told him, "Mom died today," but Jonathan felt numb. David came home not long afterward.

Dad left Mom's body in the den for several hours and asked each of the boys if they wanted to see her. Jonathan was too shaken up to answer one way or the other and simply followed when Dad led him there. She was half her normal size, a shriveled figure that seemed to have closed in on itself. David took his sketch pad and pencils and made a drawing of her.

Sarah came home later that afternoon and met Dad at the door. "He was crying," she told me when I asked about that day. "I'd never seen him cry before. He wasn't capable of saying anything. He just opened his arms and hugged me, which I also can't remember him ever doing. He was kind of broken down in a way I'd never seen him before."

She recalled the mixture of relief and emptiness in our house. "It was an emptiness that went beyond immediate activity," she said. "I really felt that the core of the family had fallen away and there was nothing to replace it." All afternoon Samson howled, making a low rumble that sounded unlike any noise he had ever made.

I never cried for my mother. With the resiliency of a child, I absorbed the loss and kept going. Yet her absence touched every part of my life. And it set in motion all the events that later separated our family.

In time and space, she is a distant presence from me. I have only a handful of memories. But when people ask me what I remember best about her I don't have to hesitate a moment before answering: the food. I think of stew pots of thick split-pea soup simmering on top of the stove on a long winter day, bubbling around a rich ham bone, and how it steamed as she ladled it into bowls and tore off hunks of a long baguette. I think of trays of warm cookies with gooey chocolate chips emerging from the oven at the same moment I stormed inside, soaked, from romping through the snow. I think of metal beaters and flat, plastic spatulas coated in sweet, sugary cake batter handed to me for a thorough licking. I think of bowls of beef soaked in barbecue sauce, platters of French toast and peach kuchen, plates of matzo brei sprinkled with sugar, bowls of carrots flavored with orange juice and brown sugar, handmade matzo balls in steaming broth. I know that all the best and sweetest food I have eaten or ever will eat in my life was consumed before I was eight years old. For years after my mother's death, I would have sudden and vivid memories of some dish I hadn't eaten since I was five—her spoonburgers, for instance, a kind of sloppy joe that she and the other moms made once a year and brought to my elementary school in Washington for hot-lunch day.

I think of the sound of an old Olivetti typewriter clacking away in some distant corner of the house, a sound that meant my mother was working, hunched over the table, a stack of yellow paper and carbons beside her. I remember her old desk, its cubbyholes crammed with rubber bands, paper clips, stamps, and occasionally a pack of cigarettes, its drawers jammed with envelopes and papers. I remember the books lining the walls of her den and the way they darkened the room, and the wicker shoulder bag on her closet floor, which overflowed with back issues of *The New York Review of Books,* and the menagerie of owl paperweights and statues lining the windowsill. I remember the way this awesome room bespoke seriousness and made me think about becoming a writer. There was something romantic and exciting about her life, the books and papers and arguments and comrades. In a way, I think we all wanted to become writers because of her.

I think of her massaging Vicks VapoRub across my chest and tucking in my blankets at night, of the aggravation in her voice when she felt my neck and wondered if I had come down with the mumps. I think of the birthday when I asked her to leave all my gifts outside my bedroom door the night before and she did, and the Christmas when I asked for a tent and my parents set it up in the living room and stacked my other presents inside, and the Halloween when she dressed me in ragged clothes and stuffed my limbs with straw and sent me as a scarecrow to a costume contest.

I think of the timbre and tone of her voice, which I can capture inside myself and remember precisely, even though I can't recall any one specific thing she said.

My mother's death prompted an outpouring of love and affection. Dozens of readers wrote of their sorrow to the *National
Observer*. The newspaper devoted pages and pages of a special
issue to her work. Writers, editors, and old friends wrote to
my father. Obituaries appeared in *The New York Times* and *The
Post*. For weeks, it seemed that every time we opened our front
door we found another coffee cake wrapped in tinfoil on our
doorstep.

Hundreds of people attended her memorial service at
Georgetown University's Dahlgren Chapel. They played Cat
Stevens's "Morning Has Broken" and tapes of my mother
speaking; they read from her poems and journals and the
Psalms; they placed objects that were symbolic of her, like her
glasses, on the altar. A number of people who attended that
event still remember how moved they were by it.

I didn't fully know what was going on. I missed her, of
course, but I thought the funeral was long and kind of boring.
I didn't know many of the people who were speaking. I sat up
front with my family and played with a little plastic carrot, an
Easter toy. When I flipped open the lid of the carrot, a white
bunny's head rose up like a jack-in-the-box and squeaked. Steve
watched me enviously from his seat, where he had to sit still
with his parents and behave.

One morning a few weeks later, the whole family drove to
Nova for its long Easter mass. That was the morning we scattered my mother's ashes.

I don't remember much about that morning, but I do

know my father wanted each of us to participate. The service began before dawn, with a group of chilly, tired people huddling outside in the darkness for songs and prayers. Most people held a flickering white candle, with wax dripping down onto their fingers.

After a while, we were marching in a procession. I could see the sun starting to come up. A breeze lifted our hair and made our coats flap like flags. We stopped three times before mountainous piles of wood. At each one, someone lit a fire. I was carrying a small black box. Three times, the priest dipped his fingers into the box, and held out his hand, to let the wind carry away the chunky, chalky lumps of ash.

SEVEN

❧ ❧ ❧

My mother's death left us fractured, numb, raw, but also relieved and feeling guilty for being so. Each of us retreated into his own private world. When we began to drift back together a few weeks later, we were like immigrants in the land of survivors, living in a completely new landscape. It seemed to me as if the members of my old family had been removed and replaced by exact replicas: the same but different.

The center of this new family, my father, was poised and calm during those first days. Though we children were grieving, he had done much of his mourning while Mom was dying. He tried to be generous with his time. He stayed home from work for several weeks after her death. He accompanied me when I embarked on the insane mission of going to every classroom at my school and inviting all the teachers, even those I didn't know, to her funeral. He carefully clipped her obituaries, bundled them with the program from her funeral and some of the letters he had received about her, and compiled memory books for each of the children.

But for all his control, when I look back today, I think of

my father as a compass gradually losing its magnetism. Out-wardly, he took my mother's death so well that at times it almost seemed unnatural. I never saw much open sorrow. But I instinctively grasped that in the slower way he carried himself, in the silent sadness of his gestures, he was not the same man.

I was only dimly aware of some of the troubles weighing him down, of course. But on almost every front, he faced small crises. He had recently left the police department and started a new job, which he had barely been able to perform because of his wife's illness. While trying to address the needs of his children, he was wondering what to do about his own. An essentially solitary man, he had just lost not only a wife but one of the few people whom he had ever let get truly close to him. Midway through his life, he faced the task of reinventing himself. For all his achievements, it was intimi-dating without my mother.

"You must understand, that all those years I lived with your mother, I never considered myself to be that bright," he said to me once, as we talked over those days. "I always con-sidered your mother to be superior to me. She was a brilliant person. After she died, I was kind of drifting."

The new job, at the federal Civil Service Commission, quickly turned out to be a horrible mistake. As an evaluation manager, his main duty was to inspect regional personnel operations for the federal government. It was supposed to be a prestigious position, even a step up from his previous one. But he hated it. He had no office of his own. In addition to the problems with his boss, his two immediate subordinates were feuding with the rest of the office. The work wasn't very interesting, and he didn't think he was good at it. Most of his coworkers were career bureaucrats who specialized in infighting. He still worked long hours but was irritated by the demands of this dull and frustrating post, especially compared with the excitement of the old one.

On weekends he dabbled in personnel consulting, an offshoot of his days with the police department. He traveled to Milwaukee, Las Vegas, and Denver, where he led workshops and gave speeches on hiring to various law-enforcement agencies. But he gradually came to see it as grueling and shallow work. He wasn't readily remembered for his time with the Washington police. "I remained animated by the same issues that had fired my early days in the police department, such as hiring women and blacks," he said. "But the managers I met increasingly seemed more concerned with the bottom line. They weren't going to do something unless it was required by law."

In the evenings, meanwhile, he set out to build a new personal life. Bizarrely, he registered for dance classes and began going out two or three nights a week to learn the tango and the fox-trot. He tried to pick up writing plays again, rejoined his writing groups, started reading in the living room late at night, a dish of ice cream and pound cake on the ottoman before him.

Early that summer, he called some of his acquaintances to see if they knew any single women. Soon he was dating regularly for the first time in his life. Over the next several years, he introduced us to a string of women who came to the house for dinner. He brought home a high school guidance counselor who talked to us as if we were all four-year-olds, and a schoolteacher with a daughter who lived far out in rural Virginia. He went to concerts at the Kennedy Center and movies and restaurants across the city. He attended an inaugural ball for Jimmy Carter. It all felt liberating, a chance to do a lot of different things he had never done before. For the first time in his life, he began to see himself as attractive. Once when he went to a dating service, the woman in charge told him she wanted to date him herself. Often he came home from work just long enough to say hello, change, and head out again. Sometimes he didn't return until early the next morning.

His most serious involvement was with a Texas woman with two nearly grown daughters who worked on Capitol Hill. A pretty brunette who always smiled and spoke with a lilt, she was feminine and glamorous in a way that my mother hadn't been. She tried to make friends with me, for instance, obtaining for me the autograph of a man she knew who was an actor on a soap opera, even though I had never heard of him. But I could tell she wanted ultimately to marry my father and discipline me. I crafted a cutting imitation of her Texas drawl and amused my friends with it. I even wrote an essay for my English class ridiculing her. Dad and she maintained an on-and-off relationship for several years.

One of the consequences of Dad's new life was his decision to quit Nova. Nova was largely populated by couples, some of whom had nearly worshipped my mother. He didn't fit in so well anymore. Some members thought he was angry at the church for what had happened. But falling away was less a conscious decision than the natural consequence of his affairs.

For all his efforts, though, dating proved less satisfying than he had hoped. From time to time he talked about getting married again, and occasionally I found myself imagining what it would be like for one of these women, and maybe even some odious step-sibling, to move in and stake a claim on our lives. But he never spoke very seriously about it, and I doubted he would marry any of them. My mother had been right when she predicted he wouldn't meet anyone who measured up to her. "Your mother was my best friend, a vivacious, vital person that would bring a lot of color into my life every day," he told me. "None of the other women I dated could measure up. They all paled in comparison to her."

And through it all, he drove himself hard. One morning while he was driving the car pool to work, he stopped at a red light and began to doze off. His foot slipped off the brake and the car shot out and nearly rammed the bumper ahead. The other people in the car eyed him as if he were falling apart.

※ ※ ※

Around the house, we noticed the effect of the new regime almost immediately. The clocklike efficiency with which my mother juggled her chores and writing became a distant memory. Dad's first load of laundry dyed our underwear pink and left mysterious green stains on the sheets. When he started fixing my sandwiches in the morning, I had to tell him not to put butter on the bread. The fridge was filled with cookies and soda pop and all the snacks my mother monitored as carefully as ration tickets. Being out of the house so much, Dad didn't have much time to keep things clean. A lot of the daily work devolved on my sister, who was paid a weekly allowance of ten dollars to dust and vacuum. Because Dad often worked late, he recruited the children to rotate making dinner. My sister ended up doing most of the work, but for a while I ate a lot of my brother's spaghetti sauce. Within a few months, we mutually let the formality of family dinners slip away anyway, each of us eating when and what he wanted to on many nights.

Not a very experienced cook himself, Dad gamely set out to prepare his first big family meal a few weeks after Mom died. He settled on lasagna, which seemed a safe but pleasing choice. He drove to the supermarket with a list and checked off the ingredients. He read and reread the recipe that afternoon. Anticipation passed through the hallways: Dad is going to make his first meal. In late afternoon, he took up residence in the kitchen, gathering the materials on one corner of the counter. He moved slowly, deliberately. He preheated the oven. He layered the noodles in the pan. He browned the ground beef and scooped it on top. He spread more noodles, the sauce, the cheese. He slid it into the oven and watched it brown through the little window.

Finally, triumphantly, he carried it to the table, where we four children sat waiting. It looked beautiful, too good to eat. The cheese was perfectly browned.

He served up portions and handed out plates. Someone took a bite. There was a sharp crunch.

Was lasagna supposed to make a noise?

It was my sister, already a better cook at thirteen than any of us would ever be, who realized the error: Dad hadn't known to boil the noodles before they went in the pan. They were baked but uncooked. We went out for Chinese.

To his credit, he maintained a sort of plodding, happy-go-lucky geniality that warded off such potential humiliations. He laughed at his own ineptitude and joined in our teasing. He strove merely for equilibrium and gradually shaped the routines of the house to his schedule. He started rising in the dark every morning to put away the dishes; the clanging and banging downstairs would invade our sleep. He came to my room to wake me and said a quick good-bye at the table before he ran out to meet his car pool. He scaled back his expectations in the kitchen, learning to prepare simple but nutritious meals: canned carrots and baby peas heated on the stove, barbecued chicken baked in the oven, lettuce heads separated into bowls and garnished with radishes. He didn't fuss about the house constantly being clean. He signed my report cards and took me to the dentist and over to Sears to buy new clothes. He obtained the names of some baby-sitters from mothers in the neighborhood. He packed up my mother's papers, bought new office supplies, and took over her den, sitting at her big work table to pay bills and work on his plays. He politely and patiently explained what had happened to the callers who asked to speak to "Mrs. Murray," until they finally stopped telephoning.

Beyond the mundane household tasks, he had to figure out how to go from being a part-time parent to become both mother and father to four children. He wasn't too worried about the two oldest boys, who were just about grown. But his daughter was only thirteen and acutely aware that she was now the only female member of the family.

And I, a seven-year-old who didn't quite understand what had been lost, was his greatest concern. He knew that in raising me he would have to make key decisions that he hadn't made for the other children. But he also knew he wasn't going to become a full-time father.

Especially during the first year after Mom died, I wanted him around all the time. I don't blame him now for the urgency he felt in plunging back into the world, but at the time I did. My father was the one member of the family whose presence under our roof made me feel safe. Being placed under the care of a baby-sitter or a sibling relegated me to second-class status. One night while he was out on a date I sat up writing him a letter to tell him how miserable I was that he was out so much. I left it on his pillow so he would be sure to find it when he came home. He told me years later that the note devastated him and added to his confusion and sense of shortcomings. That was what I wanted to hear.

I soon got used to being alone. Frequently the house already was empty by the time I came downstairs for breakfast in the morning. Within a few weeks of Mom's death, I had discovered that no one would ever know if I decided to skip a bowl of cereal for breakfast in favor of an ice-cream sandwich. I was given a piece of string with a house key to wear around my neck, so I could let myself in. I often came home to an empty house in the afternoon. I learned to content myself by listening to records in my room, reading a book, or, increasingly, sitting in front of the television. At night no one asked me if I brushed my teeth or looked for dirt behind my ears. I was asked to do very few chores and received very little criticism when I did them poorly. It was easier for my father to take the garbage out himself when he got home than badger me about it. Occasionally I would guiltily offer to help clean the dishes after dinner. But I did a halfhearted job. My father would have to sneak into the kitchen later in the evening, remove them from the drying pan, and rewash them to remove the greasy film.

I quickly figured out that if Dad was a friend and a comforting presence, he was not able, maybe not even willing, to be much of a traditional parent. He seemed to have abdicated the responsibility of training me, assuring my good character, and keeping me in line. In all the years after Mom died, he tried to discipline me precisely three times. Twice he banned me from watching what he saw as inappropriate television shows, which I watched behind his back anyway. The third time he spanked me for a temper tantrum at the dentist, but it was such a feeble effort that after a few minutes, I just looked up and asked, "Are you done?" We both realized he didn't have it in him to do it again. Beyond those episodes, all of which occurred within eighteen months of Mom's death, I'm not sure I ever even heard him raise his voice.

To make up for his frequent absences, he seemed to have decided to be my benefactor, defender, and friend. "I had made the decision right away that I was not going to be a slave to the family and have no other life than that," he once told me. "So, when your mother died, I pondered how to raise you from that point on. I was so busy in my job and my extracurricular activities that I couldn't raise you the way your mother did. So I decided I was going to try to show you love, and that's what I set out to do. I tried to convey it in everything I did. I fumbled around and tried to do the best I could."

The unfortunate side effect of this was that I became spoiled and bratty. I was soon watching as much television as I wanted and learning from the box the arts of sarcastic commentary and comic timing. I became an expert joke-teller and learned how to torment my siblings and friends, even my teachers, with a running commentary of wise-guy remarks. An avid reader of children's books under my mother's tutelage, I quit reading almost altogether for close to five years. The only books on my shelf were collections of "Peanuts" strips and editorial cartoons.

Within a year, I had developed an afternoon routine. I would come home from school, head right for the kitchen and a snack, then carry my food and my books upstairs. There I settled into the enormous yellow beanbag chair I had been given for Christmas and flicked on the black-and-white portable television I had gotten for my birthday. The afternoon was devoted to Bugs Bunny and Superman. At five, reruns of old sitcoms like *Gilligan's Island* and *My Three Sons* came on. At eight the prime-time shows started, and I sat watching all of them, too. Television events marked the milestones of my life, while the characters inspired some of my deepest emotional commitments. I saw Gloria give birth on *All in the Family* and James die on *Good Times*. I tried to dress like Bobby Brady. For years, I imagined myself as the star of America's most-watched TV show and pretended my daily routines—walking to school, doing my homework, going to the bathroom—were fascinating storylines that I, the most beloved and popular boy in the nation, was acting out.

My diet went steadily downhill. My mother had watched my food intake like a hawk. No matter how busy she was, she always found time to sit at the table after dinner and wait for me to finish eating my spinach. Dad was a significantly softer touch. He bought just about anything I added to the shopping list. By the age of ten, I was drinking four or five Cokes a day. I lived on frozen pizzas, Otter Pops, beef jerky, steak sandwiches, Doritos, chocolate chip cookies, and the only vegetable I would deign to eat: canned corn.

Eventually I gained so much weight that I grew self-conscious about it and persuaded my father to come with me to Weight Watchers. One evening he drove us to an office building in Bethesda where a meeting was held in the basement. There were maybe a dozen women there, most of them in their thirties and forties. We were the only males weighing in that night, and I was the only child. They seemed pleased and slightly amused that we had come. I checked in at 135. The group talked about watching themselves on dessert for a few minutes. They applauded a woman who had lost three pounds. When it was over they gave us some little booklets about dieting, some recipes, and a little scale on which to weigh food, and invited us back. For a short time I tried diligently to measure my calories, while Dad learned to skin chicken parts and cut back on salad dressing. Naturally, only he had the discipline to maintain the diet for more than a few weeks; I soon lost interest and reverted to my old habits. Dad said nothing about it.

My most passionate interest was probably my comic-book collection, and that inspired what was, in its way, a special ritual for me and my father. A friend had discovered a treasure trove of comics in a store about twenty minutes from our house. It was one of those nerd havens whose shelves overflowed with comic-crammed cardboard boxes and little plastic figurines from *Star Trek* and Dungeons and Dragons. The proprietor was an arrested adolescent, a gaunt, gawky, awkward man with a bad haircut, thick black glasses, and an aversion to looking anyone in the eye; he stood behind a crowded counter fourteen hours a day, six days a week, discussing Spiderman's romantic mishaps with twelve-year-olds. After I became a regular, this man, whose life I wanted, informed me that the new comics arrived every Thursday afternoon and that the store stayed open into the evening to cater to the screaming hordes of greedy preteens such as myself. This could not be ignored.

I laid it all out for my father: I wanted my allowance Thursday, and I wanted it raised to seven dollars from five so I could afford the many titles I read. In exchange, I would never ask him for another thing for as long as I lived.

He agreed. And so on Thursday nights he started coming

home from work a little early, changing out of his suit, and driving us to the store. In the car, he took out his wallet and let me count out my allowance. While I maniacally rummaged through the bins and racks for an hour or more, he would patiently wait, leaning against an old cardboard box filled with back issues of *Cracked* magazine.

Despite my earlier agreement, I regularly feigned amnesia and asked for a little extra spending money. Wanting to make me happy, Dad always obliged. Though I'm not proud to say it, I became almost a little extortionist. For letting him live his own life, I wanted funds to amuse myself.

Over the years, Dad bankrolled me through a host of phases. When I wanted to be a comedian, he bought me dozens of record albums to study, from Bill Cosby to Steve Martin. After I sat up in my room, memorizing the routines, he obligingly laughed when I went downstairs and performed them all for him.

When I wanted to be a magician, he discovered a magic store where we bought card tricks, Chinese linking rings, stuffed rabbits, fake thumbs, silk scarves, and small foam-rubber balls I could hide in my fist. He agreed that I needed a hat, a wand, a cape, and small pieces of paper that you could set on fire and flash for effect. On a trip to New York he took me to Tannen's Magic Studio in Chelsea and spent a hundred dollars on tin cans with exploding snakes, an elaborate house of cards, and even a small wooden stage. He sat in the living room while I fumbled through a little routine.

When I wanted to collect fish, he bought me a ten-gallon aquarium, a lid with a light, a filter, little bits of charcoal, gravel, little porcelain treasure chests, and clamshells, algae, fish food, snails, a big plastic hose with which to clean the tank, and a half-dozen fish. He welcomed a parade of cats through the house and more than once had to sit me down to tell me one had been hit by a car. When I saw a beautiful Shetland sheepdog at the pet store, Dad agreed to bring him home. When I lost interest in the dog after a few weeks, he patiently took over the feeding and the walks, and even sent the dog to obedience school to bring him under control. But the dog became increasingly neurotic anyway and started shredding books and barking incessantly. Dad finally bought a huge chain, attached one end to the dog's collar and the other to a tree stump, and banished him for most of the day and many nights to the backyard. Finally, while I was at school one day, he took the poor thing away. I came home to find the house empty and quiet. Secretly relieved by what he had done, I nonetheless screamed and cried and called him a tyrant.

He supported me through a disastrous series of efforts to learn an instrument. I loved the idea of being a musician but lacked the discipline to practice every day or learn to read music. Yet he paid for instruments and lessons for the violin, drums, and the banjo, each time told me how well I was doing, and didn't protest when I inevitably announced that I was giving up.

Indeed, remarkably, he kept most of his opinions to himself. I won't even attempt to tally up the movies, chocolate bars, bowling trips, bubble-gum balls, rock concerts, birthday parties, and fast-food meals he financed. I can't even remember all the one-shot expenditures, like the time I had to write a paper on Robert Browning, when my father drove to five different bookstores around Washington until he found one where he could buy the complete, three-volume set, consisting of thousands of pages of Browning, so I could consult one poem.

I knew at the time that I was taking advantage. But so did he. Years later, he told me, "I never worried about your getting spoiled or becoming bratty. I figured you would outgrow those traits. What did concern me was that on my own I would prove to be a poor substitute for two parents. I had very ambiguous feelings. I didn't want to hurt you, but I didn't want to turn my life over to you. I have some lingering guilts about my role and relationships during those four or five years after your mother's death. I probably could have done better."

And somehow we became uniquely close. As the house started emptying out, Dad and I increasingly were thrown together. He took me to see the Washington Bullets and to the circus with my friends. We went to the movies and to a nearby steak house for dinners out. He treated me and my friends to trips to the amusement park and huge pizza parties for my birthday. He took me on vacations to Disney World and Niagara Falls, even brought my friend Steve along so I would have someone to play with. When my brothers and sister complained that he was spoiling me rotten, he brushed them off.

If my childhood was different from those of my friends and siblings, if I was known in school as the boy whose mother had died, and if I sometimes tired of coming home to an empty house most afternoons, I also knew that I had a father who instead of being angry when he caught me imitating him laughed, who welcomed my friends over to play at any time, who came home when I called him at work and let me take sick days without making much of a fuss. When my friends complained about their fathers, telling stories about being grounded, getting yelled at about homework, and shouting matches that erupted over dinner, I never had any stories to share, as they well knew. My father was so easygoing that most of my friends spent as much time at our house as they did at their own.

For all his failures and my frustrations, I knew that love surely threaded all he did, even if he was too generous and even if I did not fully understand and did not at all appreciate it. On some level, I knew my father spoiled me in a clumsy attempt to set things right for a boy whom he felt had been cheated by life. I understood that this was the way he conveyed his feelings. The gentle look in his eyes, the smile, the willingness to drop everything for me, said that he somehow wanted more than anything just for me to be happy.

⚛ ⚛ ⚛

A few years after Mom died, we were an entirely different family. David and Sarah were gone. Most of our family obligations had fallen by the wayside. There were no longer any rituals everyone was expected to follow, no requirements of conduct toward one another. We had taken our last family vacation in the summer of 1975, when Dad rented a beach house, and even then we had each brought along friends of our own to hang out with. Each year, the five us had sat down to dinner together less often, until it became a rare event when we did so. By that time, I was so used to eating in front of the television that I made it seem an incredible inconvenience to drag myself to the dining room table. Any sense of parental discipline had gone out the window.

The greatest thing we had in common was probably a desire to pursue new lives, and that included my father. While he had enjoyed some of his experiences, he was feeling increasingly dissatisfied with himself. He felt a lack of depth in his life and in what he was doing. Everything seemed to be drifting away. Four years after his wife died, he remained acutely aware of the shadow she cast and felt that he still didn't know what he was supposed to do with the rest of his life.

Around the time he turned fifty, he wrote out a list of the things he disliked in himself and wanted to change, ranging from the superficial to the substantive. He wanted to enjoy himself more and be more emotive. He wanted to shake off some of the trappings of middle age in his wardrobe and tastes and be a little more modern. He thought about getting a new job, maybe becoming a consultant full-time. And he wanted to sort out some of his unresolved spiritual questions.

At some point, he quietly, almost subconsciously began to feel as if he was groping in the dark for an answer to his unhappiness, some clue to the way his life was going to turn out. Looking over his list, trying to figure out what to do, he pondered two questions over and over. First, what do I do about all this? And, second, how do I get from all of these things to where it is I really want to go?

EIGHT

❋ ❋ ❋

I don't know if anybody can be converted without seeing themselves
in a kind of blasting annihilating light, a blast that will last a lifetime.

—FLANNERY O'CONNOR

To my father, it was all very simple: In 1979, when I was
turning thirteen, he fell madly, passionately in love again.
With God.

He explained this to me one frigid morning as we sat in
one of the two guest rooms at Saint Bede. They are located
beneath the monastery's main lobby, along a cool, dark, quiet
hallway, up the corridor from the studio of Father Joseph,
the artist, and the TV room, from which you can sometimes
hear laughter emanating late at night about the time that *Sein-
feld* reruns come on. Sunk halfway underground, the rooms
are usually freezing at that time of year. But Benedictine
monks are famous for their hospitality, and the accommo-
dations reflect that. The rooms are compact and tidy, with
carpeted floors, single beds, chairs, desks, a row of fifteen-
year-old religious books with titles like *Prayer: Our Journey*

Home, modern bathrooms, and a cabinet full of toothpaste and other complimentary toiletries. Across the hall, in the den, the guest master, Father Marion, keeps the minifridge stocked with cans of Lite beer and diet Coke, and leaves big, plastic-covered bowls of pretzels and Chex mix in the cupboard.

My father and I faced each other from hard, straight, cloth chairs, bracketed by my unmade bed on one side and a floor lamp on the other. The chairs were so uncomfortable and I was so restless that as we talked I kept stretching my toes on the floor and tipping mine back. A fingertip of morning sunlight crept between the slats of the blinds.

I told him I wanted to know about his conversion. I had lived with him during that time but nearly twenty years later did not know much about his experiences. I had seen the changes in the outward man without grasping the inner transformation. There were many things I didn't understand and many questions I had never asked.

He answered every question in a clear, calm voice, so serene that it seemed to belie the fantastic—to say the least—nature of the events he described. As he spoke, he struck me as being something like a war veteran, one of those men who comes home when the fighting ends and resumes his old life but who has lived through struggles that have irrevocably changed everything he was and colored his view of the world, such that his loved ones can never fully understand.

The first prospect of early retirement for my father arose in the late fall of 1978. The Civil Service Commission was to be abolished in favor of three new agencies, and all employees who had worked for the government at least twenty-five years had the opportunity to retire. Counting his years in the Army, my father just made the cut. He was sorely tempted to get out but still unsure of what would come next. He was only fifty-two years old.

One of the things he had always wanted to do was attend a religious retreat. In keeping with his efforts to reinvigorate his life, he decided now was the time. He called around until he found someone who recommended a Franciscan school in Virginia with fourteen or fifteen brothers. He signed up for a retreat in March, with the intention of spending it thinking about whether he should retire.

The evening he drove out, he had trouble finding the monastery. It was a simple-looking building, and he sailed right past it, then had to turn around and go back. The place was dark. No lights shone even in the driveway. He knocked, but no one came. He checked the address again, looked around the driveway, and then just walked in. There was a sign in the lobby reading GUESTS. He went inside the room and started to unpack when a brother appeared and told him, "That's not where you go, you're in some other place." The brother took him to the chapel where the monks prayed, pointed out where the visitors would sit, told him what time to get up, then led him to his room.

Always an early riser with an innate desire to please, my father arrived at the chapel early the next morning. It was the first time he had tried to pray in years. He sat down and closed his eyes. "I was prayerful," he said. "It felt good being in the dark with all those brothers." He heard people shuffle past him and take their seats. He was very curious to see the abbot and occasionally peered at the group around him wondering which one was in charge. Finally he heard an authoritative pair of feet striding through the doorway and down the aisle, accompanied by one or two other sets of footsteps. The robed monk nodded at him as he passed, and he thought to himself, "That is the abbot."

After prayer, the group silently made its way to the refectory for breakfast. It turned out that the solemn figure who had started prayer was the cook. "When the cook came, everything was ready, and prayer started," my father recalled.

"So, I prayed with them. I went to mass with them. I spent a whole weekend reading spiritual magazines. I read like twenty-six of them. I had a hell of a good time. And I came back from there with the intention that I would start going to church again."

He searched for a church in our area and found Holy Cross five minutes away. He made an appointment with the pastor, Father Lewis, and made a general confession. The following Sunday he went to mass, and he never missed it again.

"I received the bread and wine, went back to my pew, and knelt down. And this tremendous gush of tears flowed. That was the beginning of my gift of tears. And I kept saying over and over again, 'Thank you, God, for restoring my feelings,' but I didn't know what I was saying. I just kept saying it and saying it and saying it. The tears kept coming and coming and coming. And then that was the beginning of it. Over the next few months they came sporadically. That summer, for example, we were at the beach, and I went out in the water up to my waist in the early afternoon, and the sun was streaming down. And I stayed there for half an hour. And the tears came again. I had that experience several times over that summer."

He retired on June 30 and began attending daily mass the next day. "I had a certain desire and fervor to do it," he said. "It had been building up over that spring ever since I'd been on the retreat. It just felt right."

He quickly developed a routine. "I would get there early. I'd get there as soon as the church opened and be there an hour before mass. I knew many of the standard prayers from when I was a kid. When I would go to church before mass I would sometimes say vocal prayers and sometimes I would just be silent. I just was in the presence of God. And I'd be there after mass. Within weeks I was invited to be a Eucharistic minister and a lector. Then the assistant pastor asked me if I'd teach CCD that fall. Within several months, I was invited to join a couple of prayer groups. So I quickly got involved in the affairs of that parish."

Soon the tears were coming almost every day. "At the elevation of the host, the tears would come," he said. "I went for perhaps four or five years experiencing tears perhaps three hundred sixty out of three hundred sixty-five days a year."

He wept so frequently that finally he went up for communion one day and the pastor refused him wine. He approached

Dad afterward and told him he was afraid people wouldn't want to drink because they would think tears had gotten into the wine. Dad prayed about that and concluded that on weekdays, when there were only a handful of people at mass, he would get at the end of the line and take wine last. On Sundays, he would skip it altogether, so he wouldn't cause a scandal.

"This was a humiliating experience for a man to have this happen," he said. "When the tears started coming every day, people reacted in strange ways. This one Sunday, this woman I'd never seen before came up after mass and sat down and said, 'What is wrong with you?' Turns out she was a religious—a sister from someplace visiting relatives. She said, 'Are you sick? What's going on here?' I calmly explained to her about the gift of tears, which I had begun to learn about, by reading and talking to people."

He was learning more about the church in those early months but was confused. He still was influenced by life in the secular world and unfamiliar with many of the terms and ideas he encountered in this slightly alien one. He started buying books recommended by people at church and reading them hungrily to figure out what was happening to him. He very quickly made friends with other regulars at the church. What he learned, he said, was that "I had never really understood my faith, or really had deep faith. I was a nominal Catholic. I was ignorant. I thought I knew a lot, but I understood very little about the religion or about spirituality or about relationships with God at all."

As the tears intensified, he began letting himself go in

prayer. That seemed to make him more peaceful. "At some point, I wasn't in command. I abandoned myself to God. From 1979 on, I really have made no decisions. I've been led every step of the way in prayer." It was fearsome, he said, but the desire was strong. "It was a leap of faith to trust what would happen. The first time you have these experiences about letting go, it is difficult. You really are uneasy about it. Of course, that's what faith is all about. If you are a person who wants to control the future and wants to have a rational explanation for everything going on in your life, you are not taking a leap of faith. A leap of faith is when, in spite of everything I know, everything I've experienced, everything I believe, in spite of man's sometimes inhumanity to man, in spite of evil, in spite of sin, in spite of my own failings, in spite of all these things, in spite of what a person does to me, I do it anyway. It's like a child who on the second story of a building opens the window and plunges down in the expectation that his father will open his arms and catch him."

Hadn't you been that kind of skeptical person? I asked. He nodded. "In my jobs, I had the ability to be given a task, a challenge, and I would be able to get the big picture. I knew what it took, and I had the expertise to get there. When I converted, I no longer had control over myself or where I was going. Each day I would wake up and take one step after another and be led. It was a radical transformation."

But didn't you fear you were having a breakdown? I asked. Didn't you consider seeing a psychiatrist or some kind of counselor?

He shook his head. Early on, he said, he was convinced through his prayer, reading, and talking with people that the tears were a sign of spiritual turmoil but not psychological problems. "I never had a fear I was having a breakdown. I was peaceful about the whole experience. I just abandoned myself to God." He eventually concluded that his tears were a cleansing gift of joy, not sorrow, and that all he could do was accept them. It all sounded very simple.

❋ ❋ ❋

He was still dating that summer, but by late August he had given it up and decided to become celibate. He called the Texas woman, whom he had been seeing again some, and let her know what was happening. He told her they could remain friends but that there was no possibility of sex. She protested that they would be good friends forever and said a cheery good-bye. He never heard from her again. He wrote another letter explaining his decision to a woman he had recently dated for the first and only time. She called him on the phone and shrieked at him and asked him what was the matter with him and whether he had seen a psychiatrist. He calmly explained again what was happening. Three days later she called him back for spiritual advice.

He thought it likely he would marry again but planned to remain chaste until he met what he calls a "holy woman." He also expected that he would remain in his role with the family, and that we would be included in whatever decisions he made. "You children were not excluded at all. You were a part of what was going on in my life. I did not see a conflict there at all. I did not start out on the conversion experiences to become a priest or a monk or anything else." But he admitted that he handed over to God questions about our future. "I just had to yield with what I was being taught and the way I was being led."

Did you regret that? I asked.

"It was very hard," he told me. "But I just had to be peaceful with what was happening. I tried not to make it an issue within the family."

By the fall, his church life was taking up much of his time. Besides dating, he had given up writing. He burned his plays one afternoon and even hounded one playwright into giving him a refund check for a writing course he had decided not to take. During that time he also began reading my mother's journals and reflecting on their life together. He found a passage written about seven years after their marriage in which she said she doubted he would ever be a writer. It was a bit hard to take. "I prayed about what my writing had accomplished," he said. "The understanding I received was this: It was a small boat, which served the purpose of taking me to a given shore, which I had now arrived at. It was a means to an end."

In the first weekend of October, he decided to go on another retreat, with some men from the parish, to a place in rural Maryland. While there, he met with the Jesuit priest who was the director of the weekend retreat. He was curious about the sacrament of reconciliation—confession, as most people think of it. He started to tell the priest about himself and what had been happening to him, when the tears started flowing. They lasted perhaps two minutes, during which he couldn't talk. The priest sat quietly, then began asking him about himself. He told my father a little about the sacrament, then asked him, "Have you ever been on a directed retreat?" My father didn't know what that was.

What the priest was proposing was a full-time retreat, usually intended for people who are already advanced in spiritual exercises, under the guidance of a spiritual director. A director, akin to but not the same as a counselor, is supposed to listen to a directee's story and assess, in my father's words, whether the messages being received come from the God, the self, or the devil.

The program followed at the retreat center was designed by Saint Ignatius of Loyola, a sixteenth-century Spaniard who also had the gift of tears. Ignatius's spiritual excercises are divided into four weeks of intense meditations, each of which is built around a theme. The first week is meant to evoke sorrow and contrition for one's sin in the interest of purifying the soul; the second and third weeks derive mostly from the public life and crucifixion of Christ; and the fourth focuses on Christ's resurrection. Ignatius demands specificity and concentration; the complicated exercises ask deeply personal questions, require almost constant self-monitoring, and even recommend essays and diagrams of sin. Their stated purpose is "to gain mastery over one's self and to live a well-ordered life not making life choices that take shape from disordered effects." One is almost continually meditating on sin, Christ's sacrifice, and the meaning of life and is asked to interact directly with Christ. You can meditate for five hours on one passage of the Bible. I can only guess at what such a retreat is like from the inside. But even to read the exercises is intimidating. They set out to scour your mind.

It turned out that my father had been looking at a book on Saint Ignatius in his room and thought the exercises sounded appealing. But he couldn't take the usual thirty-day retreat because of his family. So the priest agreed that he could break the exercises up so he could work at them three times a day at home for several months and come meet him once a week.

That is when he started going down to our basement to pray. "You didn't know what was going on," he recalled. "You had no idea. It was during the day while you were at school. I did not share it with people." Outside the basement, he tried to live his life as normally as possible. He was around a lot now because he had given up dating. But most of his time and energy went into the exercises. He was doing three hours of biblical meditation a day, and he loved it. "I found I had a natural affinity for this sort of thing. I took to it like crazy."

He started to have a series of what he would later call "mystical experiences." One day, he told me, he was in the basement doing the hourly exercise and the hour ended and he didn't want it to be over. So he just sat and prayed. Suddenly, he remembered that during the trip to New England that spring, when we had stopped to visit the priory in Vermont, we had been in the gift shop when I had picked up a rosary and asked him what it was. After he told me, he recalled (I have no memory of this incident) that I said to him, "You need to buy this."

So he did. He brought it home and dropped it in a drawer and forgot about it. Now he was seized by an impulse to go get the rosary, come back to his chair, and start saying it. He said the prayers, and the instant he was finished, Christ was in the room with him. He did not see Him, but he felt an overwhelming, loving presence that left no doubt. There was a burning sensation in his heart. It was awe-inspiring. It lasted for twenty-five minutes.

That experience changed his life for good, he told me. He consecrated himself to Mary and began inviting her to pray with him, a practice he has never abandoned. He has said the rosary almost every day since then. "That was the key experience. It opened my heart. I was a different person. I became more charitable. I became more interested in people. Until you begin experiencing it, you don't believe it, it's so amazing, but it happens to people. It's not something you understand in your head. It's something you experience." He now considered himself to be living in the presence of God, not metaphorically, but in the actual physical sense. It was a feeling that never again left him.

There were similar experiences that month. For one exercise, while meditating on what kind of king Christ was, he felt him instantly there washing my father's feet. That encounter, with the humble, servile Christ, was the whole revelation. I laughed nervously as he remembered it.

Not all the exercises were so easily accessible to him. Ignatius lived during the late Middle Ages and held medieval views of some matters. He described hell in the literal, physical imagery of the age, and to Dad it seemed like something from a comic book. He had never spent much time thinking about heaven and hell, but he couldn't see hell in Ignatius's terms. So he asked himself: What could it be? "A place without hope, a place without love. The devil was not one person sitting on a throne but a person of a thousand disguises. As I went on, I found myself able to elaborate very great details of what hell was like."

A couple of months later, while he was still doing the exercises, the priest from the retreat center suggested he go out to another town in Maryland and attend a parish retreat. At the end of the first full day, a Saturday, there was a five o'clock mass, and the retreatants were supposed to pick out two or three people, approach them, and ask them for prayer. Dad went up to a nun and one or two other people and told them, "I want you to pray for me that I've been forgiven for my sins." Just before mass started, an old lady came up and asked him to pray for her, so he asked her to pray for him, too. During the mass he had an almost continuous flood of tears. That evening, the woman sought him out, took hold of his hands, and told him, "My dear, I prayed as you asked me to during the mass. There's no question that your sins have been forgiven and God has a very special mission for you."

Because he had broken them up so he could stay home, the exercises ended up running from October through February. During those months, Dad began to display the unusual intensity that he would henceforth bring to his religious life. Toward the end, the priest wanted him to pick out passages on a biblical theme and meditate about them. He chose about two dozen of them. The next week he started going through them and the priest suddenly got very unsettled. Listening to Dad, he began to get the idea that he was thinking of becoming a priest. He cut him off and snapped, "I didn't ask you to do all of this."

"He was feeling self-conscious, as if maybe he had led me astray and that I thought I was going to become a priest," Dad said. "It was really comical. I said, 'I've just been going where I've been led, and I don't have any thoughts about it one way or the other.' He said, 'Well, it's not a good life, you don't make much money, you wouldn't be able to raise your kids.' I said, 'Well, I'm just trying to go where God wants me to go.' But he was very upset by that experience."

When the exercises ended, the priest recommended a new spiritual director for him, one in Washington. This one, also, was a Jesuit.

※ ※ ※

Under the guidance of the new director, Dad dabbled in charismatics. This movement, rooted in the Protestant evangelical sects of the nineteenth century, focuses on the Holy spirit and the emotional side of spirituality. Members take turns offering up spontaneous prayers and sometimes speak in tongues. Dad liked some of the people in the prayer group he joined but sometimes felt very strange at their meetings. "If somebody starts babbling in a foreign tongue and nobody can interpret it, I don't know what advantage there is to it," he said. "Sometimes people have this gift of tongues and they're speaking in a language they don't even know they know. Saint Paul talks about this gift, and it is a legitimate gift. That kind of thing can happen. But some of the times it would just seem gibberish to me." He stayed with the group, on and off, for about two years.

He was almost totally subsumed in his new life by this time. He had given up secular reading, watched little television, and spent as much time as he could praying and reading. For his second Lent back in the church, he suggested to his new director that they pick a few people in the community to meet once a week and meditate on the Passion. They ended up in a group of eight, who met regularly at one another's houses.

The night Dad hosted (I'm sure I was squirreled away in my room with the TV on, avoiding everyone), he suddenly felt drawn to one member, a beautiful, black-haired Polish woman. He realized there was chemistry between them. She was taken with the house, especially the paintings my parents had collected. She seemed impressed by the way Dad led the service. "I was attracted to her, but I didn't understand this attraction because after I stopped dating and started to lead a chaste life, my understanding was that I would one day find a holy woman to marry," he recalled. He was confused because, though he felt she was holy, she had been divorced, which meant they wouldn't have been able to marry even if something did develop. The reason she gave for divorcing her husband was that she needed to spend more time with God.

All that week, he mulled over the situation and prayed for guidance. On the night of the next meeting, he arrived early. He pulled up to the curb, turned off the engine, and began to pray again. Suddenly he heard a voice, which said, "You are to treat her as if you were a priest." He kept a distance all that night. The next morning at mass, he heard the same voice again, while praying. It told him, "From this day forward, you are to regard yourself as being a priest. I will take care of the details in my own good time." He met with the woman and told her what had happened but didn't do anything else except pass the story on to his spiritual director.

Shortly after that, Dad and the director began to have problems. "He wasn't too happy with the direction in which I was going," he recalled. "I didn't want to end the spiritual direction with him, because I had been led to him. However, after one particularly tense meeting between us, I happened to be rereading Teresa of Avila's autobiography at a place where she was having difficulty with her spiritual director. Her clear advice to laypeople was: Sometimes you are better off having no spiritual director than the wrong one. I took it as a sign." He broke his ties with the priest.

He doesn't remember sitting down to talk to me, though he says it makes sense that he would have. He wasn't sure where he was going or how it would affect the family. "At the heart of conversion experiences you're shutting out all the things you see in your life that are less important than God, and you're focusing on God," he told me.

In a sense, this meant not thinking about the family. Instead of making decisions about us, he was trying to cede them to God. This was part of a larger struggle for him to give up control.

"I was aware that you children did not understand what was happening, but I really feel I gave myself to all of you during those years. I did try to be involved. As you recall, at the time, none of you children were religious. There was no way I could have explained these experiences to you so you would have understood them. The only thing I could do was be a witness to you. Jonathan for a time thought I was off my rocker. He thought I was going to go to my ruin."

If he had any regrets, he said, it was that he and Mom hadn't raised us in a more rigorously religious manner. As time passed, he felt separated from us by a gulf of misunderstanding. "I was very sad that you children had not gotten the education and experiences of God that would have prepared you for that happening to somebody," he said.

❊   ❊   ❊

Early in 1982, nearly three years into his renewed religious life, he had the idea that he was meant now to be more active as a Catholic. He made an appointment to go to the Catholic Worker office in downtown Washington. It was on Nineteenth Street, in the middle of a bad neighborhood. He followed the directions to the office, walked through a big door, and found himself in a room filled with mostly middle-aged women who were smoking and wore rouge and lipstick and paint on their nails. It was a brothel, but he didn't realize that until later. One of the women asked him how he had gotten in. He had entered by a side door. She asked what he wanted. A bit nervously, he answered, "I'm looking for the Catholic Worker." They were suspicious of him, but someone finally gave the directions. It turned out to be the building next door, on the second floor.

He spent the day there but left discouraged. "It was an oppressive environment," he recalled. "There were two women working in the office. One was in her late twenties. She was the office manager. The other, in her thirties, was the assistant. I was told there were two priests who lived there at night and went away to other parts of the city during the day for their ministries. The office manager was near a nervous breakdown. I was indignant with these priests, because these two women were so stressed and the priests were not properly ministering to them. After I left, I went home to pray about whether I was to get involved. It felt wrong and uncomfortable. I wondered whether I was being called to that kind of a life. It just didn't seem to fit with my family or anything else."

Two mornings later, he was leaving mass when a woman followed him out. He recognized her as a regular who usually sat across the aisle from him, but he hadn't met her. She told him, "I've got a message from God for you." He introduced himself and invited her over for coffee. After they sat down, she delivered her message: "God wants you to stay here and keep doing what you're doing until you hear further from him."

So he waited and started looking for a new spiritual director. A friend recommended a priest she knew in Canada, some-one he and Mom had met years earlier during a vacation. He wrote him, and they began corresponding.

Around this time he had decided to sell our house and shed his possessions. He was unsure he would stay in Washington and didn't want to be burdened. He had no problem getting rid of our old things. "I'm not a person who lives in the past," he said simply. But once we moved, money became a worry. He had calculated how much he could pay for rent after he gave up the house but ended up taking an apartment that cost two hundred dollars a month more than he could afford. He had misgivings about it, but since Sarah was back home and we kids had such mixed feelings about moving to an apartment, he decided to take a place that would make us comfortable. After we moved, he started piling up debts on credit cards.

One benefit of our move, however, was that he could now walk to church. "I was very involved in the life of that parish and with the friends from there," he remembered. "It was a very rich, whole life." He was fasting extensively. He would eat just two simple meals every other day. In a few months he lost about twenty pounds.

He began to think he might become a diocesan priest but still didn't have a clear sign. In the spring of 1983, he wrote to the Washington archdiocese to ask about the priesthood. He heard nothing for weeks. Then a mutual acquaintance mentioned my father to a classmate, who was secretary to the archbishop. He discovered the application had been mis-placed. He called Dad for an interview, and was so enthusi-astic that he said he would recommend to the archbishop that Dad begin studies in the fall. But after praying, Dad wrote the man the next day, saying he did not think God wanted him to be a priest in the Washington archdiocese.

Still, he was feeling a growing urgency. Late that fall, just after I had left for college, his spiritual director wrote him that he thought he should make a move. Still waiting to hear from the archdiocese, Dad applied to a Connecticut seminary he had seen advertised, one that sought older candidates. He drove up for an interview in February. It seemed to go well. The priest who vetted applicants there told him he needed to take a routine psychological exam, which was set for May. He decided that if they rejected him, he would leave home, go to Canada, and see whether he should join his spiritual director's community. He was restless and itching to do something.

But he had an uneasy feeling. "During Holy Week that spring, on Holy Thursday, Good Friday, and Holy Saturday, I experienced the worst three days of my life," he recalled. "I suffered from beginning to end in every conceivable way. My nerves were shattered, my skin had sores on it, I itched. During the course of the three days it was made very clear to me that I would be rejected at Holy Apostles and in Canada."

In May he traveled to Connecticut for his interview with the psychologist anyway. In July he found out he had indeed been rejected, though he was not told why.

By that time, he had broken the lease on the apartment and sold or given away most of the rest of his belongings. My sister moved out to California. I was away at college. He felt ready to move on and confident that the Lord would direct him.

It was at this point that he started staying with friends while he figured out what to do. His spiritual director was upset with him for his rashness and discouraged him from traveling to Canada to join his own community. Dad started looking around for something else.

A priest at Holy Cross parish had heard of Saint Bede and encouraged Dad to apply there. He wrote a letter to the then-abbot, Abbot Marion, but received a reply that was not very encouraging. Dad's letter had been couched in terms of priesthood, but the abbot emphasized that one must be in the community several years before the abbey would even consider the question of the priesthood. "He described the length of the process leading to solemn vows. First, you were a postulant for a minimum of several months; then a novice for at least a year; then a junior monk for at least five years. I got the impression that he thought, at my age, it was dubious at best." Still, the abbot invited him to visit.

Dad drove out from Washington in early September, thinking of the trip as little more than a courtesy visit. He stayed in South Bend, Indiana, with friends, then set out for Peru on a Monday morning. Eight miles from the Indiana border, his car broke down, on a busy highway. He sat in the car quietly reading a religious book. After about twenty minutes, two men walked up and offered to push him to the side of the road. They told him that state troopers did not come along very often so he should walk down a ravine by the highway to make a phone call to get towed. A tow truck came about twenty minutes after he called and took the car to a Volkswagen dealer. Dad paid the tower forty-two of the forty-eight

dollars in cash he had. As the dealer got to work, Dad told
him he did not have enough money or credit to pay for the
work. But the dealer did the work anyway and had the car
ready to go by early afternoon. He took two of Dad's charge
cards and made out two bills under fifty dollars each, so he
could get by without calling the charges in. Then he sent him
on his way.

He arrived in midafternoon. One of the monks, Father
Benedict, was working in the fields, and he came and took
Dad into the monastery and called the vocation director. "I
was taken to my room, on the first floor," Dad recalled. "The
door opened to a new life. All was tranquil. All was right.
The community proved to be gracious and hospitable. I was
asked to stay a couple of extra days." Of course, he added, he
was amused to discover that the abbot was almost the same
age he was.

After he drove back east, Dad boarded with several sets of
friends and waited. Saint Bede wanted him to find out why
he had been rejected in Connecticut. He discovered the psychologist had found his tests inconclusive and had suggested
more testing, but the seminary had simply rejected him.

That autumn was probably the nadir for our family, and
he told me that he felt great anguish during those months.
"I still talk about the fact that in college you had no place
to go and how much pain that caused me," he told me. The
Christmas of 1984, the same one I spent alone waiting for
the bird to die, he was staying in the house of some friends
who had gone away to their vacation home. He was entirely
alone. "I got no phone call, no card, no gift from the children,

or anybody. I knew I had caused this myself; because of the fact that I was moving around, I didn't have a permanent address, didn't have a phone number. But I also suspected there was more to it than that. There was some kind of feelings on the part of the children, and they were mixed. Jonathan had the hardest time when I broke up the home—he really wanted that home there so once or twice a year he could come home and be there. It bothered me very much that he was so upset."

Just before Christmas, he was invited to return to Saint Bede for a month in March. He had a sense it might work out and decided to take a monthlong Ignatian retreat in January to prepare. Every day he wrote copious notes on his prayer life and reading. He meditated on a revelation given him to say to a priest: "Do not be afraid to look unblinkingly into the eye of love." He stopped by a chapel to pray one day and had tears for fifteen minutes. "By the time it was over I knew that no one had ever loved me like that—no human," he wrote. By the end of thirty days, his notes had accumulated to more than nine hundred pages. It was clear both to him and to his spiritual director by then that he was going to end up in a religious community rather than be a diocesan priest. But it was also clear that he would be a priest.

At the end of the retreat, he asked the spiritual director if he had any prophetic words to offer. The director thought for a while and then told him, "You are going to be a great preacher."

"It startled the hell out of me," he recalled. "I don't have much of a voice, I did not even know then if I was to be at

Saint Bede. He said I had a wide-ranging mind and could cull all sorts of references from life and from the Bible."

Now six years into his new religious life, he had no home, very few possessions, and almost no close ties with his family. But he still felt the price was worth paying. "I did not see my future as being a fading parent who was going to stay around fifty-two weeks a year for the times when my children were going to come home," he told me. "I just couldn't see myself in that role. And while I felt bad about the family, I was not really concerned with the lack of understanding of me from you kids. That was the Lord's to take care of. I really abandoned myself to God and trusted in God and put myself in God's hands."

※ ※ ※

They struck me as slightly cold words. Yet I was comforted, too, to know that what I had seen as mystifying, at times disturbing behavior, was in fact my father's own attempt to answer the same questions I was starting to ask in those years. It stunned me to know how much he had kept hidden from me, not out of his own embarrassment but out of a desire not to embarrass me.

But there was no getting around the questions that went beyond our parochial family concerns and right to my heart, and about those I didn't quite know what to say. What can you say, really, when your father tells you he once encountered Jesus Christ in your basement?

My instinct, if it was anyone but my father speaking, would

be to wonder about his sanity. I'd think he might as well have sat down and told me that last night he'd lain in a tent wrestling with God or an angel until dawn and then gone home and founded a nation. I'd think he should be off in an airport selling flowers.

I'd point out that, in my daily job as a writer, I deal in a world of facts and known quantities. I live in a city and work and socialize in circles where most people doubt the existence of God, to say the least. Many are suspicious of religion, seeing it alternately as something that only their parents cared about, a right-wing plot to curb personal freedom, or an out-dated series of superstitions that is the province of fools and charlatans. At various times in my life, I had been more than willing to subscribe to one or more of those explanations.

And yet, from time to time, something insistently whispers to me: God exists. Beyond logic, perhaps, that voice, after receding for years, has slowly gotten louder as I have gotten older and other ways of living and being have proved unsatisfying. Like most people I've met, I want there to be something more than the everyday world. Maybe I want to believe everything my father says so I don't have to consider the alternative. But unlike him, I haven't been granted the gift of tears or given visions of Christ. My voice refuses to speak with anything approaching the boldness or certainty of the one my father says he heard. It doesn't bother to answer various theological objections or manifest itself in any other form. It doesn't speak loudly enough to persuade me to live the life of a good Christian. It only sends out its message like a line—steadily, insistently, but faintly.

I rarely do much about it. But it is there. It stands as a challenge to me. What does it mean if I say that, deep down, I believe? Do I believe in a God that can do anything? And if I do, why does that make the story my father told me seem, well, deeply weird? Wouldn't all he told me be not only possible but perfectly reasonable?

I look at the man across from me. He is happy, sane, peaceful, fulfilled, far more than he was twenty years ago. People flock to him, love him; a palpable spirituality emanates from him. I not only love him, I like him, too. There is no doubt that he is at peace with himself and the world.

Isn't that some sort of evidence?

PART THREE
THE HOLY SPIRIT

NINE

※ ※ ※

I reached Joliet, Illinois, late one broiling August afternoon. It was the usual dispiriting jumble of fast-food restaurants, strip malls, and tract housing. I had been driving all day from Pittsburgh with the air conditioner blasting into my face, but it wasn't helping much. My hands stuck to the steering wheel. All I wanted was to find a cheap hotel room and a hanger for my blue linen blazer, which was wrinkling in the backseat. I was supposed to wear it to a baptism the next morning.

I hadn't bothered booking a room in advance, because I knew Joliet had more hotels than it needed. But there was no room at the Days Inn, or at the Ramada, or at the Holiday Inn. At the third hotel, the clerk warned me that every place in town was probably full. At the fifth hotel, I asked the skinny teenager behind the desk what was going on. It was the casino, he said. It had just opened. Every weekend now, people poured in from downstate Illinois, Indiana, and Missouri to gamble.

I was now tired, hot, and aggravated with all Midwestern gamblers. I was sick of driving and sick of traffic. It looked like I probably couldn't find a place to stay. I sat in the parking lot, idling, wondering what to do next.

An idea began to take shape in the back of my mind. I thought of a place where I could go. It would be another hour out of my way, but there would surely be a room for me there.

I filled my gas tank, turned up the radio, and steered back onto U.S. Route 80. Driving into the sunset, I whipped past a flat expanse of cornfields, tree groves, and cookie-cutter housing developments till I reached the exit I was looking for.

Off the highway, I followed a path that's become familiar to me in recent years. I suppose I know it as well as any route I take. It's not as comfortable to me as, say, the drive to the house where I grew up—that trip is like a part of me—but I know the landmarks as well as points on a map.

You drive through the outskirts of Peru, Illinois, along Illinois Route 251, past the Steak 'n Shake, then the Peru Mall and the Wal-Mart. By the lumber store, you turn right and drive a few blocks, passing flat houses of stone, wood, and brick, then the rolling hills of the city cemetery. Finally you break free into open land, alongside fields of corn and soybeans. To the left, you can see a cluster of red-brick buildings in the distance, with a bell tower rising from the plain like a lighthouse: your destination. At the end of the road you turn left. You cross U.S. Route 6, drive by a large placard reading ST. BEDE, and enter a narrow driveway lined with pine and flowering crab apple trees.

The road takes you straight toward a big, U-shaped building, covered in vines. It looks a little like a college dormitory. It turns right, then circumvents the far end of the U, where a new building of brick and glass stands. On the other side, you drive through a small grove of white pines, then into a cramped parking lot.

Silence washes over the car. You can hear the faint trickle of a fountain, the chirping of birds. Overhead, the bright red ball of the sun sinks slowly, casting a burnt-orange glow on everything below.

I stepped from the car and walked into the small, bricked courtyard at the top of the parking lot. To my right stood an old, imposing building, fronted by steep stone steps leading to a heavy wooden door. To the left was the brighter, cleaner addition, with modern glass doors. Over my head stretched a walkway connecting them.

No one ran out to greet me. No one ever does. As always, the place seemed deserted.

Looking around, I noticed that a light was burning in the high window on the second story to my left. I checked my watch: 7:25. The monks were at prayer. I would have to wait awhile.

I plopped down on a swinging bench. I was tired, but it felt good to be here. Fireflies winked past me. A cool breeze whistled along the grass and slid up my leg. My breathing slowed. I thought to myself: If God is anywhere, He is surely here right now.

Pulling up to the doorway of this Catholic monastery always seems strange yet strangely comforting. It's a little like arriving at the entrance to a foreign land and a little like coming home. The old place, with its creaky floors, dark corners, and cavernous halls, has become familiar to me. I have grown used to the soft tones and deliberate but slightly distant demeanors of monks. They have tried to make me feel welcome here.

But comforting as these environs have become, it feels, too, as if I have stepped out of the everyday world and entered a different one, lost in time. The silence is inviting but at the same time oppressive. Everything conspires to make you feel calm, then to unsettle you. You feel like there's no place to hide.

People had been forming monasteries for thousands of years before the birth of Christ. Christian monasticism rose in the third century in the deserts of Syria and Egypt, as the Roman empire began to crumble. It was Benedict of Nursia who defined the framework that made Catholic monasteries one of the most important institutions in the European Middle Ages. Benedict is a murky figure; the version of his story that we have today is a mix of hearsay, history, and hagiography. The son of a Roman nobleman, he was sent to Rome to study as a young man in the late 400s but was reportedly dismayed by the vice and corruption in that city, which already was under the thumb of barbarian kings. He gave up his home, devoted himself to the single-minded pursuit of God, and retreated to Subiaco, about thirty-five miles away, where he spent three years living in a cave above a lake. His only human contact for most of that time was with a local monk who occasionally brought him food and clothing. He wore animal skins that frightened local shepherds. He once rolled naked in nettles to purge himself of lust.

Benedict's piety gained the notice of a group of local monks who invited him to be their leader—after they poisoned their former abbot. Understandably wary, Benedict agreed to take his place, but his own rigorous asceticism soon irritated his charges and they decided to poison him, too. When Benedict blessed the cup in which the fatal drink was offered, it is said to have shattered as if struck by a rock. Taking this as a sign from God, he left the monastery and returned to his former home. The miracle is Benedict's most famous; the shattered cup appears in the bottom left corner of the Benedictine medal, which is carried by most monks in his order today.

Many other miracles were attributed to Benedict. It is said that he could read people's minds and make water flow from rocks; he even once sent a disciple to walk on water. As his fame grew, he attracted dozens of apostles, who formed monasteries under his guidance. But his growing power and influence also inspired jealousy. To scandalize Benedict and his followers, a rival priest hosted an exhibition of naked women dancing in the courtyard of one of the monasteries. Worried that he was becoming a divisive presence, Benedict decided to leave the area and start anew.

He settled at Monte Cassino, near Naples, and founded a new monastery on the site of an old Apollonian temple. It was here that, drawing on several existing rule books, he wrote down the instructions to his monks, which became one of the most important documents in the history of the world. The Rule of Benedict spread across Europe and had become the standard at most monasteries by the time of Charlemagne. The period from 550 to 1150 is sometimes called the "Benedictine centuries." Throughout the Middle Ages, as European monks preserved the heritage of ancient civilizations in scriptoria, pressed wine in vineyards, preached to the poor, taught Latin to students, and received huge endowments of land and money from nobles, they aspired to live according to the Rule of Benedict. The Rule survived periodic assaults on monasteries—including Benedict's own, which was sacked by Lombards thirty years after he died of a fever in 547—and the Protestant Reformation and survives to this day. Some 8,700 men and 18,200 women currently profess to live under its precepts around the world. Among them is my father.

Even after 1,500, years the Rule of Benedict is surprisingly accessible. Though you might expect a lot of fire and brimstone in its seventy-three short chapters, it mostly preaches moderation and flexibility. Benedict lays down only a couple of absolute guidelines, including conversion through a monastic way of life, stability within the community, and obedience to the abbot. Otherwise, he preaches common sense. Brothers are urged to "try to be the first to show respect to the other, supporting with the greatest patience one another's weaknesses of body or behavior." Those going on a journey are reminded to "get underclothing from the wardrobe. On their return they are to wash it and give it back." Though "we read that monks should not drink wine at all . . . since the monks of our day cannot be convinced of this, let us at least agree to drink moderately, and not to the point of excess . . ." Benedict recommends restricting each monk to a half bottle of wine a day.

At Saint Bede you sometimes glimpse the simple wisdom embedded in the Rule at odd moments. The monks aren't permitted to speak before morning prayer, for instance. In the early darkness, they stumble in to breakfast, mostly keeping their eyes averted and limiting interaction to polite nods. The only noise is the occasional clank of a spoon or the munching of shredded wheat. "It's very wise," one of the monks, Father Gabriel, told me. "We have a lot less bickering because we don't talk till after morning prayers."

※　※　※

Saint Bede Abbey is only a century old and is only one manifestation of a 19th century revival of Benedictine monasticism. Its founders came from Saint Vincent's Archabbey in Latrobe, Pennsylvania, outside Pittsburgh. In 1861 members of Saint Vincent's took charge of Saint Joseph's Church in Chicago and set up a sort of satellite office there. In 1889 the monks in Chicago petitioned the mother house for permission to establish a new college in the Peoria diocese. That May they purchased a two-hundred-acre farm in Bureau County, about a hundred miles from Chicago, for a little less than twenty thousand dollars. The first school year began two years later, and the community was upgraded to an abbey in 1910. The Right Reverend Vincent Huber was elected the first abbot, and Francis Sharkey became the first novice. He was later known as Father Aloysius. The brothers ran a junior college for several decades, but now Saint Bede only operates a high school.

At its largest, the monastery had more than seventy monks, but today there are fewer than half that many. Most are middle-aged or older. The oldest, like Father Stephen and Father Eugene, took their vows in the 1930s, when my father was still a boy. The community has a four-story residence hall, an old school building, a gym, a football field, a large kitchen, a rectory, and the chapel and choir room where the monks pray.

As I began to explore my father's religious experiences, I wanted to know the other men's stories and learn what had lured them here. In part, I was curious to know how and why someone becomes a monk in the twentieth century. It seems an anachronism, like becoming an explorer or a blacksmith. But I also had two personal motives: to learn whether any of them had been propelled by experiences similar to my father's, and to see what kind of life he had undertaken in his old age.

As several of the men told me, what monks desire most is contained in the word *monasticism* itself, which derives from the Greek word *monos*, meaning "single," or "alone." Monks are supposed to shed the self-absorption and shallow cares of the daily world and devote themselves to uniting with God in prayer. The communal setting provides support, but the essence of a monk's life is solitary. "We're all individuals, and we don't all do the same things," one of the younger monks, Brother Bede, told me. "That's what part of this community is. You have the mix of all these different characters who are each his own person."

Under Benedict's guidelines, the monks live a rhythmic life whose seductive cadence is easy for a visitor to fall into. The day is balanced between prayer—the community gathers for prayer three times a day and mass every afternoon—work, and leisure. Most of the monks I talked to told me their days managed to be both comforting in their familiarity yet constantly presenting something new. "That is what preserves our sanity, that rhythm," Father Gabriel, who has been at Saint Bede for more than forty years, told me. "If we ignore it, the superiors call us back to it. If we miss prayers and plead that we're busy with some kind of astral business, they say, 'Oh, but the prayer is the foundation of what you're trying to do, so you be there.' I think that's what keeps us from burnout. It keeps us from obsession with work, and it's what refreshes us, that rhythm of prayer and work." Father Philip told me that prayer is "kind of a constant reminder that all of the things we do are in a sense focused and flow from our relationship with God."

The life also imposes a discipline that few but the most zealous men could manage on their own. "I'm weak," one of the monks, Father Ronald, admitted to me. "You know, I don't always want to go to prayers. If I were in my own rectory with that prayer book, I'd shuck that baby. Here, I'm with like-minded people who support you in what you're doing."

Internally, of course, the life of a monk often is a silent struggle. Monks routinely confront the questions people like me spend our lives avoiding. The daily prayers rotate the entire Psalms roughly every two weeks, so the images of worship and joy and sacrifice are constantly before them. They sometimes seem like old friends. At the heart of Benedictine monasticism is a type of Bible study called *lectio divina,* in which monks are encouraged on a daily basis to select passages from scripture or other holy readings and reflect in an almost meditative state on a word, phrase, or some other portion that seems to pulsate with feeling or meaning.

More prosaically, the life can often become monotonous. Monks are more or less restricted to whatever distractions are in the monastery itself; they can't leave the grounds without the permission of the prior. "This life wouldn't be bad if it wasn't so damn daily," Brother Bede said to me once. "You have to be the type of ordered person who can do the same thing without it becoming a routine."

The standards of success here also aren't as easily recognizable as those of the outside world. The rewards, such as they are, come quietly, in humility and holiness. "You gotta be crazy for the love of God," is the way one of the monks, Father Bernard, described it. "There have been hard days," he told me. "A lot depends on your enthusiasm. That's the key to being a monk, because you can get bored, doing the same thing, the same routine almost every day. You try to be upbeat. I look forward especially to the mass and to prayers. The mass is the greatest thing I can do every day. I've only missed twice in forty-four years of priesthood."

Many of the men of Saint Bede grew up in the area and attended high school here. Bernard, named Anthony at birth, was a farm boy from nearby LaSalle when he decided to give the seminary a try before joining the Navy during World War II. Brother Bede, who came here in the seventies, is still David to his friends and his parents, who attend mass at the abbey every Sunday. Brother George, whose mother died when he was a baby, grew up in a Catholic orphanage in Chicago and naturally drifted here when he was nineteen. That was nearly sixty years ago.

In theory, a man who joins a monastery is making a life-long commitment analogous to marriage. Abbot Roger once told me that joining a monastery is like leaving behind your old family to join a new one. He said it politely, even a little matter-of-factly, but there was an implicit message to me, too: He's ours now, as much as yours.

But as in all families, time strains the bonds. Over the decades, monks can't help but become intimately acquainted with one another's tics and quirks. Though to an outsider like me monks seem all of a piece, they constantly feel their disparate personalities coming into subtle conflict. Beneath the placid exterior, monks always seem to be watching, and sometimes quietly criticizing, one another. "To some extent, it's structured as a do-or-die sort of thing," said Brother Nathaniel, the prior. "You know, if you can't stand the guy who is sitting next to you, well, good luck. Because unless he's run over by a car or falls out of a tree, for the next—it could be eighty years—he's going to be next to you." He acknowledged that there are times when the effort seems futile but added, "I suppose that, ultimately, getting married and having a family and so on, there are a lot of unreasonable things about that, too. Any time love is involved, there are a lot of unreasonable things involved."

Brother Bede looked almost hurt when I asked him how well he got along with his brothers. "There isn't anyone here I can't say that I don't love," he finally said, with a slight trace of hesitation. "But I sometimes could think of doing without them, because they can sure make life miserable at times. But you know, I'm sure I make other people's lives miserable at times, too." Brother George told me, "Some people go by me and don't say a solitary word all day."

When I asked Bernard how the men learn to get along, he looked pained for a minute. "You gotta be tolerant," he said. "I know there have been things that people have done to me that I certainly resent. I've forgiven them, but boy, a few times I've really been hurt something fierce by some of the people. You have to roll with the punches, you have to be flexible, you can't let it get you down if you fall down or make mistakes because we're only human and that's part of adapting to religious life. Once I had a novice master who told me, 'You don't look over the faults of others, you overlook them.' I never forgot that."

To put things in perspective, Bernard told me the story of what happened when one of his fellow novices quit Saint John's in Minnesota during the early 1940s. "We used to wake up the community," he recalled. "We kept an American flag on a little table in front of the bed of the person who was to wake up the community for that week. A bell would ring at four twenty-five. So at four-fifteen every morning, Brother

Ambrose—he was the night watchman—came along and went wherever the flag was to wake that person up. Well, this one morning Brother Ambrose came in and the flag was by this empty bed. I was next to that bed. So, not seeing anybody there to wake up, he went and woke me up. He said, 'Where's Father Robert?' And I said, 'He left.' 'Why did he leave?' he says. And I said, 'Well, he didn't like it.' And Brother Ambrose says, 'Hell, who likes it?' So I never forget that, too. You may not like it, but it's good for you."

Periodically, monks will just up and leave Saint Bede. The abbey lost several members during the tumultuous sixties and early seventies. Father Patrick, who had joined in 1964, decided five years later that he wanted to take a year off to make sure monastic life was really for him. He stayed away for six. He moved to Saint Louis and found work as an administrator at a hospital. He barely kept in touch with the abbey the first year. He joined two softball teams, took up bowling, and dated several women. Only with time did he begin to miss the abbey and return for periodic visits. In 1975 he came back for good, and he took his final vows the following year. "This is where my heart was," he said.

Patrick knows most people would see his return as a sign of failure in the outside world. "A lot of people have this fiction about monks," he told me. "I was listening to the radio, and I heard a description of monks and nuns that said in the Middle Ages they went to monasteries to flee the world. A lot of people think that, and it's not true. Because I think if one is fleeing the world, they soon find they brought it right with them."

That was a recurrent theme among the monks I spoke to. "I think this is the real world," Brother Bede told me. "We're all of us called to strive for a life of unity with God. That's where everybody ends up ultimately, and that's what our goal is. It's just as real as any other means of doing that."

Again and again, I asked: Is this the ultimate appeal of a monastery, the reason these seemingly anachronistic institutions survive? Do monks have some insight that others lack? "I know whatever you know," Father Patrick told me. "But it's not a matter of mere knowing, it's a matter of living. Living a certain way of life, living your convictions. It's all one thing."

Asked the same questions, Father Gabriel, a thoughtful man who knows my father well, sat back for a moment. "I don't think the people who are here understand it," he said finally. "There's always some mystery involved. And there are bound to be times as the years go on when you say to yourself, 'What did God have in mind when he steered me in this direction?'"

❊ ❊ ❊

My father asked himself that question frequently after his arrival. When he pulled up on March 4, 1985, he was prepared for things not to work out. His shaky plan, if Saint Bede rejected him, was to go to some Midwestern town, find a Catholic parish, introduce himself with a letter of recommendation from the pastor of Holy Cross, and ask for assistance.

Once he opened that door and saw that light emanating from his room, he felt he had come home after the drama of his growing religious conviction, the uprooting of his family, and his months of wandering. But despite his relief, his trials were not over. A series of quieter tests remained for him.

Saint Bede had never hosted a candidate his age, let alone one who had been married and raised a family. There was nothing unique about those circumstances, of course. Vocations had been plunging since the sixties, and the monks of Saint Bede were well aware that many of those entering seminaries and other religious programs were older people who often had worked or even headed families in the secular world.

Yet he kept encountering skeptics. Bernard, among others, didn't think my father was going to make it. "He was leading a different life entirely, and he was used to having kids around him and a wife and was in government work and all that," he recalled. "I said, 'This is going to be hard for him.'"

Abbot Roger said of his confreres, "I think they were somewhat confused about a monk who has children. And a monk who was married. Those things just aren't what you normally think of for a monk or a priest."

During his early days, Dad's ardor, the zeal of a newfound convert combined with a touch of self-righteousness, rubbed some of the monks the wrong way. They could tell he was on a serious mission; that was apparent from his almost constant praying, especially the tears that flowed from his eyes at mass. But some admitted to me that they were put off by his missionary spirit. Impelled by what he saw as his urgent summons from God, he sometimes seemed like he was out to proselytize to everyone he met. A few wondered whether he had something else going on besides a religious commitment.

"When he was first here, I got the sense that he was out to save the world, as it were, that everyone whom he came in contact with or that he got to know he wanted to change or make better," Brother Bede recalled. "My reaction to that was we've been saved, we have a Savior, we don't need another one."

The abbot remembered, "Initially they were very confused about his tears. His intensity is something they had difficulty getting used to. This guy is really serious about this stuff."

For his part, my father worried almost constantly about his age and his debts. Remembering the voice that had promised him he would become a priest, he began wondering almost immediately when he would hear more concrete details. The monks of Saint Bede were inclined to make him wait. They wanted him to endure the postulancy, then a period of at least a year as a novice, before the matter of priesthood would even be considered. Monks wait for what they consider the appropriate time to answer questions. James—he kept his own name, for simplicity's sake—got the message that he would have to be patient. But he privately fretted that the monks would not consider a man his age for the priesthood when the time came. If not, he felt that he probably would have to leave Saint Bede to find someplace where he could. "When he came here, I think because of his management background, he had this need to confront, to keep pushing an issue until something happened," Father Patrick told me. "He's gotten over that."

The monks had to make allowances for his children on matters that had never arisen before. "You're supposed to come here and deny everything for the sake of Christ," Father Philip told me. "But at the same time, you can't take away the reality that he was a father, whose mother is still alive and whose children are spread all over the country. They are still your children, and there is still that deep emotional bond, that deep spiritual bond that has to exist. We had to define what that would be like and what that would mean. For instance, the first year he was here he got permission to leave for a week for David's wedding, which I don't think is the sort of thing you would normally grant."

His most acute conflict came over money. Dad still carried the debts he had built up back home, and while he was using his monthly pension to pay those off, he also was sending some to the children. That became an issue when his novitiate, or introductory, period ended and he was admitted as a junior monk, becoming a member of the community. He was told it had been decided that he would give up his checking account and turn over his monthly pension checks to the abbey. The abbey would then pay off the approximately $12,000 worth of debts he owed, and use his pension checks to reimburse themselves—plus interest. Once the money was fully repaid, they had decided, his money could again be sent to the four children. But my father balked, saying his children needed the money now (which was true enough). He and the abbot went back and forth for weeks before the issue was resolved, with the abbey finally agreeing to pay his debts, accept his retirement checks, and set aside a portion of his pension each month for the children. To my father, the struggle encapsulated the difficulties of entering monastic life as a father.

"It was a real trial and test to abandon myself to God and

be led to a monastery," he told me. "I had a hard time being accepted as a parent. If I had simply been a priest in a diocese, then I would have been able to keep all my money because a priest doesn't take a vow of poverty. I would have had all that money available for my children. I even could have had some of my children living with me. It would have been a much more homey atmosphere. But I had gotten to a point where nothing was more important to me than my relationship with Jesus, God, and Mary. I had to trust I was being led in the right direction."

Those early months also proved to be nourishing for him spiritually, as he settled into a new identity as Brother James. No longer feeling alone, he reveled in what Father Patrick describes as a monk's "first fervor," the early months he likens to a honeymoon. As a postulant, Dad's experience wasn't too different from a fraternity pledge. The monks assigned him busywork while assessing his spirituality and propensity for obedience. His taste for hard work and willingness to take orders surprised them. He also took correction well. He seemed to enjoy the manual labor, which is seen as an essential part of a monk's life. He pruned apple trees in the orchard and learned to use a blow torch to scrape paint off metal chairs. On his own time, he explored the back paths of the abbey, whose lands total more than a thousand acres, wandering down by the railroad tracks and the small creek where kids from the area come to drink and boat on weekends. "It was like being in heaven," he told me. "Having the Blessed Sacrament every day and taking a walk every day—it just felt great. I loved it. I couldn't get enough of it."

Father Philip, the monk assigned to oversee his novitiate, was struck by Dad's willingness to adjust to his new way of life. "When they come at that age, to a certain extent, they're fairly formed in a whole variety of ways," said Philip, who is two decades younger than my father. "They've kind of become who they are. But your Dad's ways were fairly compatible with ours, and so there weren't as many challenges as there might have been. There was clearly that intensity and that sense of having a special call from the Lord."

During his first month at Saint Bede, my father underwent a psychological screening in Chicago. It was a standard part of applying for admission to the abbey. The doctor described him as a "highly complex individual," who as a boy had filled in for an inadequate father and as a man demonstrated clear leadership skills. But for much of his adulthood, the doctor continued,

> it seems likely that Jim repressed to some degree his own vulnerability . . . the unsatisfactory balance between his strengths and his weaknesses set the stage for a kind of mid-life crisis. Since his conversion in 1979, he seems to be in a process of letting go of the tight grip he had on his own significant power to succeed. He is discovering in its place the profound depth of his need to be loved, and the value of surrender to someone greater than himself. . . . I suspect that Jim will need to face again and again his own difficulty with being ordinary, limited, vulnerable and still well loved.

In those early days, my father kept mostly to himself. Initially, he didn't maintain close ties with many friends from the outside or with his children. He didn't read the paper or watch television. He didn't know anyone in the surrounding area. Instead, he immersed himself in the monastic life. He spent a lot of time thinking about his conversion and what had brought him there. While he felt at home, he wondered why he had ended up in a small town in the middle of Illinois. "I really did not understand when I first came here why I was living in a place with no blacks or other minorities, because I spent so much of my life working with them," he told me.

In his prayer life, he subsumed himself in memories of his past failures, questions about his purpose, and the growing alienation from his children. On the cusp of old age, he found himself seemingly alone, with nothing, in the middle of nowhere. Carrying around a litany of unasked questions and a burden of devotion almost by himself for years, he had been waiting for a powerful climax to his private drama and had ended up stripping paint from chairs outside a hundred-year-old building while a bunch of Midwestern farm boys in robes looked on.

Who can say whether hindsight reveals a meaningful shape to our lives or we just convince ourselves that it does? What I do know is that out of that period of reflection came the letters to his children apologizing for his shortcomings and trying to explain what had been happening to him.

I think now of those early months at Saint Bede as a sort of release for my father, one that in some ways mimicked the pleasure he felt as a young man when he entered basic training. For ten years he had been acting out a private drama—first learning to live as a widower and single parent, then grappling with his faith and future. Now he could live it publicly but shed most of the daily cares he hated. All he had to do was pray and do what he was told. He could let down his defenses and let in the rest of the world, because he had placed himself at one remove from it.

❈ ❈ ❈

The monks could see he had a calling. Even before the end of his first month, they had invited him to return that summer and be a postulant. He eagerly agreed. But as he started trying to figure out where he could stay in the interim, the monks realized how much he had riding on Saint Bede. During his last week, Father Samuel, who as the vocation director was responsible for his recruitment, met with Abbot Marion and told him, "He doesn't have anyplace to go, and he has all his possessions with him. Why don't we let him stay?"

He became a novice the following January and a junior monk a year after that. Becoming a junior monk is the last stage before taking final vows. It lasts at least five years, at the end of which the monks hold a private meeting to decide whether a candidate should be invited to join as a permanent member. Though still conditional, a junior monk is considered seriously enough committed to merit more time and investment. In the spring of 1987 the abbot finally invited my father to become a priest.

Dad was ecstatic. The invitation fulfilled what he considered to be a long-standing promise from God. But the abbot warned him that joining the priesthood was liable to take years.

Despite his college degree, Dad needed to make up twenty hours of philosophy and theology before he could even qualify for seminary. In the summers of 1987 and 1988, the abbey sent him to classes at Saint Meinrad College, in southern Indiana, where he roomed at the large monastery. In the spring of 1989 he was handed his application to become a full-time student at Saint Meinrad the following academic year.

Even that process got tangled in complications. The application asked candidates for a short autobiography. After my father had completed that part, Father Philip, who was overseeing the process, told him that the several pages he had written were inadequate for his life story. He advised him to write as much as he needed to. My father came back with sixteen single-spaced pages, covering everything from his childhood to his career and conversion. "I strive to be obedient to God's Will and to the abbot," he wrote in conclusion. "And, I pray, may I be given the grace and the strength to begin again." He almost wasn't. Well into the summer, he learned that because of his age and long autobiography, each member of Saint Meinrad's admissions committee wanted to interview him separately. "It was a witness to how difficult it is for an older person like myself to be accepted in the system," he said.

But he made it, in time, and became a full-time student again as his sixty-third birthday approached. Over the next four years, he lived for nine months of each year at Saint Meinrad. He took classes with titles like "Eucharist" and "Method in Theology" and "Free to Love: Paul's Defense of Christian Liberty and Galatians." He thirstily sat up in the library reading and writing term papers with titles like "Catechesis on the Sacrament of Marriage: Bridging the Gap Between Theory and Practice," "Scriptural Revelations: From Joshua to Kings," and "Reflections on Contemporary American Priesthood." He wrote hymns and lamentations for class projects.

In these works and classes, he unleashed all the reading and praying he had been doing for a decade and frequently won praise from his teachers for the breadth of his knowledge. He also impressed them with the same intensity and sense of purpose he had displayed at Saint Bede. During one review, he once castigated a teacher for his practice of giving daily quizzes, which he felt unfairly skewed his grade downward. In his year-end evaluation, his advisor warned him that he sometimes intimidated the teachers.

Occasionally, he reached into his past experiences to make a point in papers. "I envision Christ's life as bittersweet," he wrote once. "He always was aware, even in good times, of what was to come. I find my life as a monk bittersweet. People come to you with their problems and often, like a grieving parent, there is nothing you can do but listen and pray."

After all those years of living in near-isolation as he explored his rediscovered faith, my father found the intellectual atmosphere and companionship of Saint Meinrad stimulating. It brought him back into the larger world. But he felt that it wasn't home. As his senior year approached, he was impatient to conclude so that he could become a priest.

In his last self-evaluation at Saint Meinrad, written in the winter of 1993, my father looked forward to his ordination in four months. "Jubilation and song!" he wrote. "It is happening! At the age of 66, after living a full life, the diverse parts of my life are coming together in such a way that my horizons are broadening, my focus is away from self to community and my disparate gifts are being drawn together. I could not imagine a richer fulfillment of my life."

That ordination day had come only two years before my impromptu summer visit to Saint Bede. The whole family had returned to the abbey, just as we had eighteen months earlier when Dad took his final vows. The bishop of Peoria had laid the vestments on his shoulders. Afterward we adjourned to a party on the lawn. Drinks and sandwiches were served. One of the monks rented a pink rabbit suit and marched around like the Energizer Bunny, banging a drum that said 68 AND STILL GOING (even though my father was only sixty-six at the time). My father had just returned to Saint Bede to spend the rest of his life. In a very real sense, he felt his life's work was only now beginning.

I thought of that day as I waited in the courtyard, alone, hoping that the guest rooms wouldn't be occupied. I had been there about twenty minutes before a parade of bulky figures in black appeared in profile in the windows of the walkway above, leaving prayer. I was not surprised to see that one of the first out wore glasses and had a rapid, vigorous stride and a slightly stooped frame. In the fading light, I could make out the white, short-cropped hair crowning his head and the tip of his full beard. He looked a little nervous, and I thought of the rabbit in *Alice's Adventures in Wonderland.*

At first he looked straight ahead as he marched up that hall. But about halfway across the walkway, he turned for some reason, saw me through the window, and rapidly waved his stout fingers at me. Oddly, he didn't seem too surprised to see me sitting outside waving back to him.

A few seconds later the wooden door at the top of the courtyard stairs swung open, and my father appeared at the doorway. He came downstairs and gave me a hug. It turned out that both guest rooms were open. I picked up my bag, and we walked inside.

TEN

✣ ✣ ✣

It is no little thing to be in monasteries and in religious
congregations, to continue there without complaining
or speaking amiss, and faithfully persevere there until the end.
Blessed are they who live there and come to a good end.
If you would stand surely in grace, and profit much in virtue,
consider yourself as an exile and pilgrim here in this life,
and be glad, for the love of God, to be considered in the world
as a foolish and unworthy person, as you are.

—THOMAS À KEMPIS

My father lives in Room 401 of his monastery, in the northeast
corner on the fourth and top floor. He moved up here after he
took his final vows, thinking that climbing three flights of
steps several times a day would be good for his health. It is a
simple room, with plain tile floor and two big windows without curtains. He keeps it as cold as possible. At the front, by
the door, are a sink and a mirror. The communal bathroom is
at the other end of the hall.

Everything he owns is inside this room. Along one wall is

his single bed, covered by a wool blanket knitted for him by a friend. Beyond it stands a desk, with the usual implements on top: pencils, papers, a basket for letters, a priestly appointment calendar marked with feast days and the proper vestments to wear, pictures of David's daughter, Miriam, and Jonathan's son, Nicholas. In the drawers he stashes a sewing kit, envelopes, gum, scissors, a penknife. On a rickety table sits a computer, donated by a parent from the school, on which he types his homilies and keeps them filed by subject matter so they can be quickly referenced. In more than six years as a priest, he has built up a database of homilies so that now he need not write so many new ones. Of all the proofs of God's favor on my father, I often think his new-found ability to use a computer might be the most persuasive.

On the wall over the desk hangs a three-foot cross with a corpus of Christ. Next to the desk is a kneeler with a prayer book and a set of rosary beads. Hung along the opposite wall are a small shelf with a couple of cassettes of religious music, a calendar, and a swatter for the swarms of flies that invade his room every summer. In the closet are his two habits, a couple of coats, some black sweaters.

Most of the remaining space in the room is crammed with books and papers. Three bookcases stand against the walls, packed with hundreds of volumes, most of which look well-thumbed and all of which are tied to his religious concerns. The subjects dominating his library include theology, Bible studies, sociology, the Holocaust, and how-to for clergy. Titles include *I, Francis*; *A Still, Small Voice*; *American Catholic*

Thought on Social Questions; *Your Sins Are Forgiven You;* and *Keeping the Love You Find: A Guide for Singles.* He also has a big file cabinet filled with articles, letters, and notes on friends and family, arranged into files with such headings as "Augustine," "Chastity," "Homosexuality," "Prayer," "Parables," "Christmas," "Evil," "Matt," and "Merton." Shoved in the back of the bottom drawer is his 1993 diploma from Saint Meinrad. A stack of books sits by his bed, too. He always has two or three going at a time. Even his bookmark is religious, quoting Psalm 27: "The Lord is my light and my salvation; whom shall I fear?"

He rises most mornings around five, sometimes as early as three. These are his favorite hours. He sleeps with the window open on all but the coldest nights. Sometimes he kneels to pray or works on a classroom lesson or a homily for several hours. Around 5:15, he washes his hands and face in the sink, puts on his black habit, and heads downstairs. He is almost always one of the first monks up. At the bottom of the steps, he flips on the lights in the narrow mailroom behind the refectory and goes in to fix several pots of coffee, which will sit on the burner all morning for the monks as they wander by. He pours some for himself in a mug given him by a friend, which reads on its side, I LOVE MY WORK SO MUCH I'M SAVING SOME OF IT FOR TOMORROW. He carries it next door to the refectory, a long room of narrow tables where the monks eat. Breakfast will have been laid out along the table in back by the kitchen staff. Often he is the first to arrive. He pours a bowl of cereal, takes a banana, crosses himself, and sits to eat and read.

After breakfast, he makes his way back along the dark corridor, walking at a slightly harried pace, tilting forward from the waist, eager to reach his next destination. Everything in the monastery is connected by tunnels, so he needn't go outside if it's too cold. He passes back through the living quarters of the monastery and then into the worship assembly building on the other side. Even as he walks, he silently prays to himself, half consciously and half from instinct, "I love you, Father, I love you, Son, I love you, Holy Spirit." Along the walkway leading to the chapel, he always stops to check the thermometer that hangs just outside the window.

He enters the choir room where the monks pray three times a day. It is a spacious but intimate room, all angles and polished wood beneath an arching ceiling. It is laid out somewhat like a small stadium. The monks face one another across the main floor, from two sets of ascending rows of seats. Each monk sits before a choir stand, which resembles a podium. In a few minutes, they will shuffle in, some yawning, all subdued, to start their day with prayer, but my father likes to arrive early, to sit in the dark and pray alone. He describes it as a wordless, imageless sort of contemplation, during which he is simply in the presence of the Lord.

Summoned by the clang of electric bells, the monks gather for prayer at 6:50. Someone flicks on the lights. They take their seats solemnly, then break the morning quiet with their voices. Each session lasts between twenty minutes and a half hour and consists of an intricate series of prayers, songs, and readings, in which the monks play off one another like characters in a Greek drama. The exercise is led by two readers who sit on the main floor; the monks take turns in these roles. They will read a verse, then all the monks will read a second, then the readers alone will do a third, and so on. The prayers are chanted in a slightly flat, steady monotone, which somehow takes on a musical effect in its rhythmic cadence. I have only sometimes felt prayerful while saying them, but I have always found them to be beautiful.

Prayers often are appropriate to the time of day. The monks might begin morning prayer by singing the refrain, "Let there be light!" and in the evening start with

> Now fades all earthly splendor
> The shades of night descend
> The dying of the day
> Foretells creation's end.

During the school year, midday prayer often is quick, but evening prayer tends to be longer, a bit more relaxed after the long day of work. The brothers are required to wear their robes in the morning and evening but are exempted in the middle of the day because they often come from work. They rush in from school or the orchards in T-shirts or worn flannel shirts, in cardigans or sweatshirts. Some have big bellies hanging over their belts. At noontime they look like suburban homeowners at a town council meeting.

After morning prayer, most of the monks return through the monastery for a late breakfast or walk past the refectory and on to the high school, where classes will soon begin. My father heads downstairs alone, to another chapel, where the Blessed Sacrament is kept. It is a tiny, narrow room, with only a few chairs, tucked away behind the main chapel. On the table at the front, beneath a dim light, sits the pyx in which the communion wafers are kept. They are taken to be the actual physical presence of Christ. Now he sits and prays for as long as an hour. He believes such contemplative prayer is important for the whole world, even if most people don't recognize it. During this time he is taken completely out of himself. Praying here, he says, puts his entire life in perspective. Sometimes he will return at night, in the dark, because his craving is so strong.

❁　❁　❁

"My world is getting bigger and bigger," my father says. "And my interests are getting larger and larger." Certainly he is as busy as ever.

After morning prayer, he frequently meets with people receiving spiritual guidance. He has believed from the early days of his conversion that he was called to be a spiritual director. In recent years he has developed a thriving practice, even counseling a few priests. He regularly writes to several dozen people, occasionally including prisoners from the state correctional facility. He still runs a prayer group, comprising mostly women from the surrounding area, which gathers every two weeks or so. Women seem to respond to him as strongly as ever.

He meets people in the front parlor, just inside the entrance to the monastery. Few of the monks know much about his private ministry, but they know that when the door to the parlor is closed it often means Father James has a visitor. To be a good director, he strives to cultivate what the gospels call "the eyes to see and the ears to hear." Following the dictates of Saint Ignatius, he listens to what the directee says about his spiritual life, and assists in what is known as the discernment of spirits. Once the student, he is now the teacher asking: Did something come from the self, from God, or from evil spirits? He has no doubt such spirits, and the Devil, exist as an actual, concrete presence.

One of his directees described for me what the experience is like. She had met Dad while on a retreat. She had been dragged along by a friend but had been toying with the idea of returning to the church anyway. Her father had just died, and the timing seemed right. She liked Dad when she heard him speak and decided to see him for confession. Dad, who will spend months organizing a weekend retreat that he is to lead, often begins the event by talking a little about his own history, and she was drawn to him because of his background. She was a single mother and recovering alcoholic and was dealing with a series of difficult relatonships. "At the time, I thought, I don't know how a priest could understand about those things," she said. "So I never before would have looked for a priest to be an advisor." After the retreat she began attending mass, and a few months later she called Dad and asked for spiritual direction. She started coming to see him every three weeks or so.

He starts each session with a prayer, then sits back and listens while she tells him what's been going on in her life. He never gives advice but does try to offer her different perspectives and suggest how events in her life might relate to God. Sometimes he recommends prayers or books to her. She told me she considers my father the only male presence in her life she has ever been able to trust. "His emotions come through, but it's not showboating," she said. "He's not charismatic. His is more of a quiet, deep faith, and I like that. You know, I like to be able to kind of sit back and let that soak in."

A few months after we spoke, she won a scholarship to a seminary in Minnesota and is now working toward a master's degree in divinity.

⁂

For nine months of the year, Dad must devote four or five hours a day to teaching. In his third year as a monk he joined the high school faculty here and has been teaching full-time since his return from seminary. He is the primary teacher of religion and marriage classes for seniors, in which they spend the year studying religion, relationships, and issues of justice and peace. It's not the work he came here for, but he has, after all, taken a vow of obedience.

About three hundred students attend Saint Bede Academy. The school stands opposite the monastery, to which it is connected by a long passageway. It is a creaky old building that looks like a high school from the twenties, with dark, wide hallways, wooden doors, and green plastic chairs attached to wood-veneered desks. Dad sets up in a classroom on the second floor, opposite the religious education office. He structures each week around a theme, with a talk on Monday and

Tuesday followed midweek by some activity such as discussion groups. Fridays are always set aside for student-produced prayer services, which require the students to write a prayer and choose readings from the Old Testament and New Testament and include a period of silence.

He gives few tests and assigns few papers. He doesn't pretend to be challenging the students with difficult book work. What he judges is how much they participate, and what he aims to do is draw them slightly out of their shells. The students' most demanding task is to keep journals, which are not graded for content, but must be submitted regularly. Their purpose is to encourage self-reflection, and he says that most students, warm to the idea and eventually open up quite a bit. At times, he feels that the students reveal too much about themselves. However, when he has suggested in the past that students stop keeping the journals and have a ceremony to burn them, they have protested. They seem to find it consoling to confide in an adult. Still, reading the journals is one of the few things that can dampen his mood.

Frequently he talks to the students about his own life. During the weeks spent on marriage and relationships, for instance, he often mentions how unhappy his parents were, or how unlikely he thought a happy marriage was until he met my mother. I get the sense that for some students his shadowy past is a matter of some intrigue, especially since it is so different from those of his confreres. Once one of his students sidled up to me and confided, "A lot of us think he was in the CIA."

It wasn't until he was ordained a priest, eight years after he first arrived, that he began to feel like he was accepted. As his dreams have been realized, and as the monks have grown used to him, he has begun to mellow. To his own amazement, he says, he has learned "how bright I am. I always considered your mother far superior to me in the intellectual thing."

He has no desire to travel anywhere else or see anything but this abbey for the rest of his life. "One of the best things I've learned is you can really work at being peaceful," he told me. "Peace is not just something like a miracle, you pray for it and it comes out of the sky, but you can really change the way you handle yourself internally."

Around the abbey, he gets ribbed for the same things we children once teased him for. "He's still very much like a bull in a china shop," the abbot told me. "He's got a zip about him. Even when he says mass everything is rush rush rush. If you want anything done, he'll do it not today, but before today." His fondness for weather, especially winter weather, is a frequent topic. "He has a habit of opening up the windows and the rest of us are freezing," Brother George told me. "That's one of his bad habits." They complain about his handwriting. Once while I was there he had posted a note on the community bulletin board outside the refectory. "I've read that three times," Brother Nathaniel said to me later, "and I have no idea what the hell it says."

He carries a full load of chores beyond his classes. Because the population here has dwindled and many of the monks are old, those who can carry extra work do so. My father cleans the showers, toilets, sinks, and floors in the second-floor bathroom every week, saying his prayers as he scrubs. He runs the spelunka, the small store—really, a closet—where the monks come for toiletries. He regularly drives over to Wal-Mart to stock up on Gillette razor blades, Mennen deodorant, and bottles of Pert Plus. For a long time he was the assistant almoner, charged with giving money or food to any poor person who appeared at the door in need. One old monk asked him a few years ago if he would put drops in his eyes, so he visits him to do so every night.

A few years ago, the abbot asked him to start up an oblate program. Oblates are laypeople who are affiliated with an abbey and seek to apply the Rule of Benedict in their daily lives. Dad recruited more than seventy of them from the surrounding area and invited dozens more friends around the country to join. He included his children in the invitations, but I declined. He regularly holds prayer meetings with the oblates at the abbey. Each month, he writes, edits, and personally addresses and mails out more than two hundred copies of a newsletter. Much as he likes meeting the people, much as the other monks commend his work in building up the program, I know that one thing my father did not expect to be doing late in life is holding committee meetings, running workshops, and writing newsletters as he once did in the government. I'm sure he came here thinking he had had enough of such activities for a lifetime. But he is known around the abbey as a good person to go to when a volunteer is needed.

"I often think he probably thinks most of us don't do enough, are not zealous enough," Abbot Roger told me. "As soon as I put up a sign that there's a retreat opening, he'll be at my door and say, 'I'll do it.' He loves to do that sort of thing. I don't think he likes to be with people that much on a social level. It's more on a mission level."

He feels that communal life is right for him, but he remains, as he always has, a bit of an outsider. Some of the monks here fall into cliques, but he usually keeps to himself. The abbey is often too noisy for him. He socializes at lunch, when talking is permitted, and sometimes joins the brothers in the TV room, especially for a basketball game or a concert. He tries to catch about twenty minutes of *The News Hour* on PBS every night with a couple of the monks, but rarely watches the local news. He finds time to scan the newspaper every day and leaf through several dozen magazines in the library each month.

When he gets his day off each month, he usually spends it alone. The abbey gives him fifty dollars and the use of a car for the day. He drives off after morning prayer and doesn't need to be back until late evening. Usually he ends up in Peoria, where he might visit the Catholic bookstore and see two or three movies. He often wanders over to the multiplex and watches whatever is playing.

He also socializes with the monks every Thursday night, when they gather for community recreation, called haustas, in the lounge. They lay out cold cuts, beer, and potato chips and have a little party. Since he came here, Dad has become a regular card player. "He's good at bridge," Father Gabriel told me. "And he's a patient bridge player. We have some players who tend to be a little excitable. And I think that's quite re-markable, because he's a man who has the potential for having a temper. You can see that."

※ ※ ※

Every afternoon he roams the grounds of the abbey saying his rosary. The prayers of the rosary are old, dating to the Middle Ages, centered on Marian devotion. Gripping the beads and walking very slowly, he will say fifty or sixty decades, though the standard rosary consists of five decades. Each begins with an Our Father and proceeds with ten Hail Marys; the rosary con-cludes with a Salve Regina and an Act of Contrition. On the Hail Marys he invites Mary to pray along. He often picks saints to join him in prayer for individual people, as well; he asks Saint Joseph, for instance, to pray along when he says a decade for me.

He says a decade for each of his children, one for his mother, and one for all his family members living and dead, a designa-tion that includes, among others, my mother and his father. He prays for the souls in purgatory and sometimes prays for some of the other monks without telling them, and he keeps a long prayer list of people he counsels, people who are ill, and other friends. Often I ask him to say prayers for friends of mine. In all, he usually says somewhere between fifty and sixty decades of the rosary, in a rapid-fire mouthing that in its repe-tition almost becomes a hypnotic chant.

Sometimes as he walks he flashes back to his past, remem-bering himself as a lonely teen walking the streets of Schenectady. He sees the stages of his life as a series of boats, transporting him on a journey that brought him to this shore.

He is in most ways completely removed from the day-to-day life of our family. He calls me every Sunday night, but usually I do most of the talking. He has met his grandchildren only a handful of times. He does not intercede in family quarrels or offer unsolicited advice. Because he is only permitted two weeks of vacation each year, our whole family has not gathered for a holiday in fifteen years.

The monks tell me how often he talks of us and brags about us. Certainly he claims to be intimately, emotionally involved with us through his prayer life. He believes his daily rosary is an active, direct intercession in our lives. "I feel like the best thing I can do for people is to pray," he told me. "I'm trying to be loving and affirming and to be a friend. But I feel it's in God's hands. I have very heartfelt, warm, loving feelings about each one of you. I'm proud of you. I want you to succeed on your own terms. I want to be accessible when you need me. That's about the best I can do."

I want to believe this, but I have my doubts. Sometimes I want him to just be there, instantly, when I need him. Sometimes I want him to pick up the phone and yell at his kids for fighting. Sometimes I want there to be a big house somewhere with all my old stuff in it set up just like it was when I was seventeen. Sometimes I want the holidays to approach and not have to think about where I will go this year. Sometimes

I think that the beauty of his conversion is that he set his life up perfectly so that he can be involved with his kids in prayer and meditation without being involved in any other way. Sometimes I want a father who has nothing in the world to think about but me.

He is still in good health, a fact that he attributes to his faith. When he visits me in New York, he is able to walk for miles without getting tired. Yet every year now, I can see him age. His bald spot has spread like a rash across the back of his head; only a few strands of gray remain. The skin beneath his neck and under his arms is increasingly wrinkled. Despite his good diet, he has grown an old person's pot belly. Sometimes, on the phone, his voice sounds thin and strained. I think about his long days—his classes, his reading, his praying, his masses, his hospital work, his counseling—and I can hear exhaustion.

Sometimes I ask him to tell me about his beliefs. He is always straightforward in his answers. He believes that when he dies he will go to purgatory. He believes that there he will undergo further purification to prepare himself to live with God. He doesn't try to imagine what heaven will be like but believes he will get there only if those whom he leaves behind pray for him. Asked whether my mother's spirit is with him, if he thinks he'll see her again, he hesitates. It's not that easy, he says. Sure, she was an important part of his life, and sure, he prays for her. But he's not a sentimentalist. After death, all will be one in Christ, he says vaguely. He quotes Jesus, "At the resurrection they neither marry nor are given in marriage but are like angels in heaven" (MT. 22:30).

When I ask him why he thinks humans must live out a lifelong test to win God's favor, he admits he cannot answer. None of us knows God's reasons, he says. He only knows that the purpose of our lives is to give worship and praise.

※ ※ ※

The monks are required to eat dinner together every night at six. "We're all expected to be at meals," Father Gabriel told me. "In these United States, there are very few families that eat together anymore. We eat together every day."

They start gathering about ten minutes early, standing behind their chairs at the freshly set tables. They don't talk, but there is noise: The moments before dinner are a symphony of clanking dishes as the monks move pitchers, pour water into glasses, rotate dessert plates, rearrange silverware. My father fusses with a coffeepot, filling it with Taster's Choice and carrying it to the microwave in the corner to heat. They fiddle right up until the abbot rushes in like a busy executive and takes his place at the head table.

All stand while the abbot issues a blessing, then all sit. One monk is assigned to be reader. He sits at the podium and delivers a Bible reading. Once he finishes, the monks begin passing food and eating like Army recruits. They serve up a basic, Midwestern diet: pork loins or chicken, corn or green beans, salad, chocolate cake. During certain seasons, my father abstains on most Tuesdays and Fridays, eating nothing but two pieces of bread and drinking a glass of water three times a day. He does this specifically for victims of the Holocaust or of atrocities in places such as Rwanda, Bosnia, and Kosovo, and for all sufferers everywhere.

The monks stay silent while the reader reads. They always hear one rule from Benedict, then an excerpt from a book. It could be religious, history, memoir, or sociology. Once they read Tip O'Neill's autobiography. The abbot watches patiently and when the last person is done eating rings a bell to end the meal. They eat fast. When I first came here, I ate slowly and dragged out my meal, so that without realizing it I kept everyone at table about ten minutes too long. Lost in my own thoughts, I casually chewed away, only to look up suddenly and see seventy eyes glaring at me in silence. I haven't made that mistake again.

❧ ❧ ❧

About twice a month my father is sent to one of the nearby churches to say mass. He loves saying mass and especially handing out the Eucharist. He doesn't weep as frequently as he used to, and tears almost never come when he's celebrating. He has presided at weddings for former students and masses for friends. Once he said mass in a funeral home filled with tattooed, bearded motorcycle-gang members for a man who had died in his forties several months after being diagnosed with cancer. Another time he delivered a homily before hundreds of high school students and their parents at the abbey at a funeral for a girl from the high school whose car flipped over while she was driving home from a party.

He takes a lot of time during the week to craft his homilies. They are learned, polished, poetic, and sometimes a little long. They read as if they were written by a man who has waited fifty years to say what is on his mind and is eager to get it all out. He believes they fulfill the writing talent he has sensed in himself since his days in the Army, and he is clearly pretty proud of them. Just about every week, he mentions to me the compliments he received for his latest one. Once I teased him, "You know, you never say to me, 'Boy, my homily just sucked this week. I was really off.'" He bristled. "I don't think any of my homilies do suck," he said, sounding a little offended.

He frequently invokes his past and our family to make his points. Once, preaching on the Holy Family the Sunday after Christmas, he said: "I don't know how well-equipped I am to preach about a holy family. As a widower with four children and two grandchildren, I look back on nineteen years of a mostly happy marriage and realize it was not a holy family. . . . If—if only I could start over again. If only Michele and I were beginning again. How much better it would be. We would do all the right things." His memory led into a discussion of the intercession of the Holy Spirit into Joseph and Mary's family, then into every family, and the need to be prayerful and put God first. He concluded, "For my wife and me, it is too late. However, I pick up the pieces. Now I am in a monastery. The monks of Saint Bede are my family. I do what I can; I strive. I also stay in touch with my children and grandchildren, keep them in my heart and my prayers. I wish I could have done better by them. But they seem willing to accept me in my new life, as I am."

I have seen him preside at mass several times, and it's always an excruciating experience. I have no doubt that to most people Father James is a pious, humble, straightforward man. On the altar, he is animated, devout, a priest clearly living the words he speaks and not just going through the motions. But to me he is still my father. I imagine him at the mall, or in the car, or at the table, not blessing the body of Christ.

One day I sat in the chapel to see Dad say the daily mass, which the monks celebrate every afternoon at five. It was only 6 degrees Fahrenheit outside, with packed, hard snow on the ground. As I sat in the chapel at dusk, the skylights rapidly darkening, I felt like it was the end of the world. There were maybe two dozen people there, seeming lost in that enormous room—fewer in number than the monks. Most of them were older people, either alone or couples.

I was nervous, as I always am before a mass at which Dad is presiding. As I waited, Brother Bede approached and asked whether I would help carry up the wine and communion wafers. I agreed but ended up worrying throughout the mass that I'd make a mistake. I'd never served at communion before.

The daily service is brief and simple, lacking the pageantry of the Sunday mass and usually the better for it. Dad stood at the podium, ringed by a half-circle of monks seated against the wall. When he held up his hand to offer a blessing, all the monks who are priests raised theirs also.

The gospel reading that day was from John 2:11, about the

wedding feast at Cana. The story concerns one of Jesus' first miracles, when he turns water to wine. He does not act until Mary prods him. He initially responds, "Woman, how does your concern affect me? My hour has not yet come." Mary persists until he acts. The wedding feast at Cana is generally seen as the beginning of Christ's public career. To my father, the story demonstrates again the importance of Mary in Christ's life. He is reluctant, hesitating. She prods him. She is the agent that enables him to begin his work.

As I watched and listened, I could see with fresh eyes how much he relished standing on the podium and issuing prayers to a largely empty room. I assumed some people there might be, like me, a little worn-out after the day, eager to finish the service and get to dinner. But my father's eyes were sparkling. When I carried up the wine, he looked right through me.

I returned to my seat and sat thinking about the gospel and looking at my father as he mumbled the familiar prayers over the Eucharist. I thought about Jesus and how much he asked, and how much my father had given up to follow Him. I wondered if I could ever believe that much, and if I did, what it would mean for my life, what I would have to give up. I tried to imagine what it must have been like for Mary to send her son into the world, knowing as she did so that she would lose him forever.

❧ ❧ ❧

I think of my father a dozen times a day, in ways I could never tell him. I sit at my desk to write and wonder what it was like for him to wake up every morning in the 1950s in New York City and peck away at his typewriter. When I go to church on a rare Sunday, I sit and think of how strange it must have felt for him to find himself going every morning and breaking down. I whisk through the subway tunnels at Grand Central Station, buffeted by hundreds of commuters, and I want to call out to them: My father used to own this place! He once worked a coffee shop in this very building, long before you, and you, and you, and I, were born! I walk over to see a friend in Greenwich Village, and as I pass by a certain building I want to run inside and bang on the doors of every apartment and tell the people who live there: My father once lived here! He was here when he fell in love with my mother! This is his place! On a trip to Washington, I ride a taxicab through the streets, passing the Capitol, the Treasury Building, the Dirksen Federal Building, and the mob of TV cameras lined up outside the Federal Courthouse, and I want to roll down the window and stick my head out and cry out to the joggers and bureaucrats and clean-cut congressional aides: These are my father's streets! Not yours, not mine, but his! He once walked through these streets, going to meetings and getting lunch and looking at the cherry blossoms, and he ruled them!

He visits me in my sleep. Recently I dreamt that it was Easter morning and my whole family was together for brunch in the house in which I grew up. It was still my father's house, but we were all the ages we are now. I recognized the old wobbly dining room table, the squeaking kitchen door, the tea cart with its dusty cups. My father was religious and was thinking of moving to a religious community but hadn't yet.

He was still just a retiree living in the suburbs. My sisters-in-law were there, as were my niece and nephew—people who were never inside that house. I felt warm and happy there, and when I woke up and remembered that the house is long gone and that my father is living in a monastery, I felt a small ache. I have never dreamed of him in his monk's robe.

※ ※ ※

I once asked my father what was most different about his life today compared with the way he used to live. "I was always thinking and doing several things at the same time," he said. "For example, I would be listening or talking to somebody, but my mind would be racing. I didn't seize the moment. I didn't appreciate the beauty and the splendor of the things around me. I didn't appreciate the weight and the mystery of the person that was talking to me. In the spiritual life you begin to be more and more in the reality of the present, and that's all we really have. It's only in the present moment that God gives us his gifts and his graces."

My father is seventy-three years old. If he lives to be seventy-nine, he will have been a monk longer than he was married to my mother.

※ ※ ※

One afternoon, I walked alone down the dirt path to the green-gated cemetery where the monks of Saint Bede are buried. It sits on a small hill overlooking a quiet field, on the edge of the forest. The monks lie beneath plain, granite headstones, in the shadow of a large crucified Christ.

It was here, while I walked among the tombstones, reading the names of strangers like Nicholas Schille and Casimir Miller and Otto Gross, that my search came to an end. I wandered about, thinking about all these men who had come here, wondering about the world to come. I thought of my mother, and the sight of my father lying on the floor when he took his final vows. I remembered the day I was baptized. I pondered all the questions I still couldn't answer. And I reminded myself of the few things I do know.

I know that nearly every morning for the rest of his life, my father will wake up early. He will shuffle down the echoing old stairs of an imposing building far out in the country, a thousand miles from the places where he grew up and lived and raised his family. He will spend his days teaching, visiting, reading, and walking. He will say his rosary, and he will sit before a small metal box containing wheat wafers, and he will offer to hundreds, maybe thousands, of people the body and blood of Christ.

One day, maybe ten, fifteen, or even twenty years from now if I am lucky, my telephone will ring and a hollow, distant voice will tell me my father has died. In the last few years, I have begun to imagine what that call will be like, as if to brace myself now, while my father is still well. I already know it will be the worst moment in my life.

While the monks toll the bell once for each year of my father's life, I will fly or drive to Saint Bede Abbey and meet my sister and brothers and their families. Returning to the abbey will feel a little bit like coming home, but I know that I will also feel like a visitor at my own father's funeral.

And I will feel an ache because, while nothing scares me like the thought of my own death, I will know that for my father, death was not something he feared but something he embraced. I will know that death held for him a promise of joy greater than anything I or anyone in his family ever offered him. I will only hope that he was right to think so.

Two days after his death, in the afternoon, the monks will bring my father's body from the funeral home to the church. They will sprinkle it with holy water and spread incense over it, then carry it to a side area, where the casket will be placed, open, so the body can be viewed. The monks will pass in a solemn procession, and the wake will continue all night long and into the next day. On the first evening, the monks will hold vespers in the church, near where my father lies. The following afternoon they will hold his funeral there. Once it is all over, they will form another procession and carry his body to its resting place.

Every night at dinner, for the first thirty days after my father's death, the monks will light candles and pray for him. His place at their table will remain vacant during that period; a small cross will be placed there. And every year on the anniversary of his death, some monk will stand up at the podium in a dining room in Illinois and remind his brothers that this was the day that Father James passed away, and ask them to remember him in their prayers, even long after all the monks who once knew him have joined him in the cemetery.

And my father will be peaceful, his soul free, having ascended like the spiraling smoke from a freshly extinguished candle, light, intangible, and ethereal. And there he will be reunited with his Savior, at whose right hand, I have no doubt, he will eternally be seated.